LEARNINGEXPRESS®'s
TOEFL®
[Test of English as a Foreign Language™]
EXAM SUCCESS
In Only 6 Steps!

LEARNINGEXPRESS®'s
TOEFL®
[Test of English as a Foreign Language™]
EXAM SUCCESS
In Only 6 Steps!

Elizabeth Chesla

LEARNINGEXPRESS

NEW YORK

Copyright © 2002 LearningExpress, LLC.

All rights reserved under International and Pan-American Copyright Conventions.
Published in the United States by LearningExpress, LLC, New York.

Library of Congress Cataloging-in-Publication Data:
Chesla, Elizabeth L.
    TOEFL Exam success from LearningExpress in only 6 strategic steps / Elizabeth Chesla.—1st ed.
      p. cm.
    ISBN 1-57685-421-3 (alk. paper)
  1. English language—Textbooks for foreign speakers. 2. Test of English as a foreign language—
Study guides. 3. English language—Examinations—Study guides. I. Title.
PE1128 .C528 2002
428'.0076—dc21   2002010030

Printed in the United States of America
9 8 7 6 5 4 3 2 1
First Edition

ISBN 1-57685-421-3

For more information or to place an order, contact LearningExpress at:
  900 Broadway
  Suite 604
  New York, NY 10003

Or visit us at:
  www.learnatest.com

About the Author

Elizabeth Chesla is a lecturer in English at Polytechnic University in Brooklyn, New York, where she coordinates the Technical & Professional Communication Program. She is the author of several books and study guides, including *Write Better Essays, Reading Comprehension Success, Improve Your Writing for Work,* and *Read Better, Remember More.* In addition, she is a content developer for LearnATest.com.

Contents

Introduction

Need to take the TOEFL exam? You are not alone. Over 800,000 students take the Test of English as a Foreign Language™ each year. More than 2,000 universities and programs in the United States and Canada use the TOEFL exam to evaluate the English proficiency of applicants who are not native speakers of English. The reason for this is simple: Academic institutions want to be sure that these applicants can read, write, and comprehend spoken English so that they can succeed in the college classroom.

► What This Book Is—And Isn't

Because your score on the TOEFL exam can determine whether or not you are accepted into an academic institution or program, it is important to prepare carefully for the exam. As you have probably noticed, there are dozens of TOEFL exam preparation books available in libraries and bookstores. Most of these books provide you with practice TOEFL exams to help you become familiar with the format of the test. But taking practice TOEFL exams will do little to boost your score if what you really need is to improve your basic English skills.

That's exactly how this book can help you. The goal of *LearningExpress®'s TOEFL® Exam Success* is fourfold:

1. To explain the format of each section of the TOEFL exam.
2. To offer specific test-taking strategies that you can use on the exam.
3. To review the basic reading, writing, and listening skills you need to do well on each section.
4. To provide exercises that help you build the basic skills and practice the test-taking strategies you learn in each section.

Building your English reading, writing, and listening skills is important, of course. But before addressing these specific skill sets, this book takes you through a review of basic study skills and learning strategies. It also helps you prepare a detailed study plan. The stronger your study skills, and the better you understand learning strategies, the more you will get out of each skill-building chapter.

Each skill-building chapter of this book includes several practice exercises, and detailed answers and explanations are provided in Appendix A. Appendix B offers an extensive list of resources to help you further strengthen your basic skills. Chapter 6 provides general information about the TOEFL exam, including notes about registration and scoring.

▶ The TOEFL Exam: What the Test Is About

The TOEFL exam has four sections: Listening, Structure, Reading, and Writing. The Listening section measures your ability to understand English as spoken in North America. If you have lived in an English-speaking country or region where the accent is different than you will find on the TOEFL exam, you may need to spend some extra time adjusting to the sound of American English. The Structure section of the exam tests your knowledge of English grammar and usage, including topics such as verb tenses, idioms, and parallel structure. The Reading section measures your ability to understand passages written in English. You will be asked to identify the main idea, determine the meaning of vocabulary words, identify specific details, and draw inferences based upon the passage. Finally, the Writing section will ask you to write a short essay on a general topic. A list of possible topics is included in the *TOEFL® Computer-Based Test Information Bulletin* and online at www.toefl.org. (For more information, see Chapters 5 and 6.)

Don't Delay—Register Right Away

BECAUSE test centers fill up quickly, you should begin the TOEFL exam registration process right away. The first step you need to take is to obtain the *Bulletin*. If you have access to the Internet, the easiest way to get the *Bulletin* is to download it from www.toefl.org. Bulletins for both the paper-based and the computer-based exams are available on this site. If you don't have Internet access, you can get the *Bulletin* from an English language center or the international student office at the university to which you are applying.

You can also send a written request to:

TOEFL®/TSE® Services
P.O. Box 6151
Princeton, NJ 08541-6151
USA
609-771-7100

Why the TOEFL Exam? Why Me?

Proficiency in English is essential if you are to follow class discussions and complete the reading and writing assignments in most college classes. In many courses, you may also be required to deliver oral presentations. And if you are applying to a graduate program, you may be given a position as a teaching assistant, which means you will be expected to help undergraduate students with their schoolwork, instruct them, and grade their assignments. In order to ensure that you can succeed even though you are not studying in your native language, and that you will be a competent teaching assistant if you are applying to graduate school, colleges and other institutions require you to take the TOEFL exam.

The TOEFL exam is administered by the Educational Testing Service (ETS®), the organization that also administers other standardized tests, including the Scholastic Assessment Test (SAT®) and the Graduate Record Examination (GRE®). Even if you have lived in the United States or another English-speaking country for several years, you still may be required to take the TOEFL exam if English is not your native language. Don't be offended—this may be of benefit to you because some schools will look at your verbal SAT score with kinder eyes if you have done well on the TOEFL exam. Look at the TOEFL exam as an opportunity to learn English better if you don't know it well, or to brush up on what you already know if you are already proficient.

TOEFL Exam Facts

- In the school year 1999–2000, more than 477,245 people registered to take the paper-based TOEFL exam, and more than 348,417 people registered to take the computer-based exam.
- TOEFL exam scores are required for purposes of admission by more than 2,400 two- and four-year colleges and universities in the United States and Canada.
- The TOEFL exam is also used by institutions in other countries where English is the language of instruction.
- Many government agencies, scholarship programs, and licensing/certification agencies use TOEFL exam scores to evaluate English proficiency.
- Native speakers of 145 different languages have taken the TOEFL exam.
- Citizens of more than 220 countries and regions take the exam.

Standardized Tests and Computer Skills

In July 1998, a computer-based version of the TOEFL exam was introduced, and the paper-based exam is rapidly being phased out. In addition to mastering the English language, students who plan to take the TOEFL exam should develop their standardized test-taking skills and basic computer skills. In the United States, basic computer proficiency is assumed in college, and many of your assignments will require computer work. Multiple-choice tests are also common in college, especially in the first year when students attend introductory or "core" classes that are required of all students. Therefore, studying for the TOEFL exam will not only help you to increase your English proficiency, but it will also enable you to pick up other skills you will find useful in college.

Scoring on the TOEFL Exam

There is no single passing score on the TOEFL exam. The institutions to which you are applying determine the minimum acceptable score. However, some colleges provide ESOL (English as a Second or Other Language) classes. If you score below what is required by the institution of your choice, you may be able to register for ESOL classes your first semester and continue to take other classes when you successfully complete the ESOL course. Alternatively, you can take the TOEFL exam again, but one of the goals of this book is to prepare you to do your best and succeed the first time around.

▶ How to Use This Book

Though each chapter of this book is an effective skill-builder on its own, you will get the most out of this book by beginning with Chapter 1 and working through each chapter. Some of the later chapters refer to ideas and information discussed in earlier parts of the book, so you may find it most effective to tackle Chapters 2–5 in order (you can read Chapter 6 separately at any time). However you proceed, read carefully, take good notes, and use your time wisely. Remember that you are already on your way to success on the TOEFL exam.

LEARNINGEXPRESS®'s
TOEFL®

[Test of English as a Foreign Language™]

EXAM SUCCESS
In Only 6 Steps!

1 ▶ How to Prepare for the TOEFL® Exam

The TOEFL exam is an important test, so it's important to be properly prepared. The advice in this chapter will help you set up an effective learning environment and create a successful study plan. You will also learn important study strategies and test-taking tips.

JULIO AND OKSANA will both be taking the TOEFL exam in a few weeks. Their proficiency in English is at nearly the same level. They have both taken the practice exams in the *TOEFL® Information Bulletin*. However, Oksana has done a few things that Julio has not. She has created a study plan, determined her learning style, and reviewed test-taking strategies. She has also been learning how to relax so that she won't be nervous during the exam. Although Julio and Oksana have about the same English skills, Oksana is likely to score much higher than Julio on the exam. And for good reason: she is better prepared. She knows what to expect on the test, how she learns best, and what she needs to study. She has been following a study schedule, knows how to tackle multiple-choice questions, and knows how to calm her nerves so she can do her best on the exam. Obviously, you want to be prepared for the TOEFL exam—that's why you bought this book. But good preparation takes a lot more than just taking a practice exam or two. That's why this first chapter is all about study skills and test-taking strategies. In this chapter, you will learn how to study, how to better learn and remember, and how to tackle standardized tests like the TOEFL exam.

▶ Part I: Study Skills

Maybe it's been a while since you last studied for an exam, or maybe you have never had to prepare for a standardized test like the TOEFL exam. In any case, you may be unsure about the best way to get ready for this important exam. How much time you spend studying each week is important. But *how* you study is the key to your success. Use the study skills described in this chapter to make the most of your study time.

Environment and Attitude

To study means "to give one's attention to learning a subject; to look at with careful attention." Notice that the word *attention* comes up twice in this definition. To study well, you need to be able to focus all of your attention on the material. So the first step is to make sure you have the right kind of learning environment and attitude.

THE RIGHT MOOD

Studying can bring you wonderful rewards. You can gain new knowledge. You can do well on tests like the TOEFL exam that enable you to achieve your academic and professional goals. But it can still be difficult to get in the mood to study. After all, studying can be hard work, and you might be worried about how you will score on the exam. You may have many other things you would rather do, or you might just have trouble getting started. These are all reasons that may lead you to *procrastinate*—to put off work that you need to do. But procrastinating can cause lots of trouble at test time. If you procrastinate too much or for too long, you won't be prepared for the exam.

One of the best ways to beat procrastination is to use a **reward system.** We all like to be rewarded for a job well done. And if we know there's going to be a reward at the end of our work, it's easier to get started. So promise yourself a small reward for each study session. For example, you might promise yourself a trip to the gym or a phone call to a good friend as a reward for an hour of study. You might promise to treat yourself to a movie after you finish a chapter in a test-prep book. Or you could give yourself a nutritious snack after you finish a difficult lesson. You can also think about the reward you will give yourself when you pass the TOEFL exam. Make sure this reward is a big one!

You can also get in the mood for studying by thinking about the short- and long-term rewards you will receive for your hard work. Keep in mind the benefits you will receive from your TOEFL exam study time:

- You will read and write better in English.
- You will understand more of what you hear.
- You will be able to apply to U.S. colleges and universities.
- You will get the education you need for a successful future.

Remember, your attitude is very important. It can dramatically affect how much you learn and how well you learn it. Make sure that you have a positive attitude. You will study, you will learn, and you will do well. Your study time will be time well spent.

Mood Booster

WHENEVER you need help getting motivated to study, try saying the following out loud:

▶ I know more today than I did yesterday.

▶ I will know more after I study than I know now.

▶ Every minute I spend studying will help me achieve my goals.

THE RIGHT CONDITIONS

You can have the best attitude in the world, but if you are tired or distracted, you are going to have difficulty studying. To be at your best, you need to be focused, alert, and calm. That means you need to study under the right conditions.

Everyone is different, so you need to know what conditions work best for you. Here are some questions to consider:

1. What time of day do you work best—morning, afternoon, or evening? How early in the day or late in the night can you think clearly?
2. Do you work best in total silence? Or do you prefer music or other noise in the background?
3. If you prefer music, what kind? Classical music often helps people relax because the music is soft and there are no words. But you may prefer music that energizes you, such as rock-n-roll. Others work best with music that has special meaning to them and puts them in a positive state of mind.
4. Where do you like to work? Do you feel most comfortable sitting at the kitchen counter? At the dining room table? At a desk in your office or bedroom? (Try to avoid studying in bed. You will probably be relaxed, but you may be *too* comfortable and fall asleep.) Or do you prefer to study out of the house, in the library, or a local coffee shop?
5. What do you like to have around you when you work? Do you feel most comfortable in your favorite chair? Do you like to have pictures of family and friends around?
6. What kind of lighting do you prefer? Does soft light make you sleepy? Do you need bright light? If it's too bright, you may feel uncomfortable. If it's too dark, you may feel sleepy. Remember that poor lighting can also strain your eyes and give you a headache.
7. How does eating affect you? Do you feel most energized right after a meal? Or does eating tend to make you feel sleepy? Which foods give you a lot of energy? Which slow you down?
8. Can you put problems or other pressing concerns out of your mind to focus on a different task? How can you minimize distractions so you can fully focus on your work?

Think carefully about each of these questions. Write down your answers so you can develop a good study plan. For example, say you work best in the morning but need total silence to work. If you have children, you would be wise to schedule your study time early in the morning before the kids are up or first thing after they leave for school. If you wait until they are in bed, you will have a quiet house, but you may be too tired to study well. Similarly, if you have trouble concentrating when you are hungry, schedule study time for shortly after meals, or be sure to start your study sessions with a healthy snack.

THE RIGHT TOOLS

Help make your study session successful by having the right learning tools. As you study for the TOEFL exam, have:

- a good English-language dictionary, such as *Webster's* 10th Edition
- paper or legal pads
- pencils (and a pencil sharpener) or pens
- a highlighter, or several, in different colors
- index or other note cards
- folders or notebooks
- a calendar or Personal Digital Assistant, such as a Palm Pilot®

Keep your personal preferences in mind. Perhaps you like to write with a certain kind of pen or on a certain kind of paper. If so, make sure you have that pen or paper with you when you study. It will help you feel more comfortable and relaxed as you work.

Learning How You Learn

Imagine that you need directions to a restaurant you've never been to before. Which of the following would you do?

- Ask someone how to get there.
- Look on a map.
- List step-by-step directions.
- Draw a map or copy someone's written directions.

Most people learn in a variety of ways. They learn by seeing, hearing, doing, and organizing information from the world around them. But most of us tend to use one of these ways more than the others. That's our *dominant* (strongest) learning style. How you would handle getting directions, for example, suggests which learning style you use most often:

- **Visual.** Visual learners learn best *by seeing*. If you would look at a map for directions, you are probably a visual learner. You understand ideas best when they are in pictures or graphs. You may learn better by using different colors as you take notes. Use a highlighter (or several, in different colors) as you read to mark important ideas. Mapping and diagramming ideas are good learning strategies for visual learners.
- **Auditory.** Auditory learners learn best *by listening*. If you would ask someone to tell you directions, you are probably an auditory learner. You would probably rather listen to a lecture than read a textbook,

and you may learn better by reading aloud. Try recording your notes on a tape player and listening to your tapes. You may also benefit from listening to programs in English on the radio.

- **Kinesthetic.** Kinesthetic learners learn best *by doing.* (*Kinesthetic* means *feeling the movements of the body*). They like to keep their hands and bodies moving. If you would draw a map or copy down directions, you are probably a kinesthetic learner. You will benefit from interacting with the material you are studying. Underline, take notes, and create note cards. Recopying material will help you remember it.
- **Sequential.** Sequential learners learn best *by putting things in order.* If you would create a step-by-step list of driving directions, you are probably a sequential learner. You may learn better by creating outlines and grouping ideas together into categories.

Think carefully about how you learn. Which is your dominant learning style? Keep it in mind as you read about Learning Strategies in Part II of this chapter.

Learning Language

WHATEVER your general learning style, most of us learn to speak and understand language best *by listening.* So as you practice understanding spoken English, *close your eyes and listen.* Let your ears do the work of understanding what you hear. The more familiar you become with the sounds and rhythms of the language, the more quickly you will learn. Spend as much time as possible around people speaking English. Go to places where you will see and hear English, such as to plays or to the cinema.

Learning to read in English takes longer than learning to speak. Fortunately, the more you listen to and speak in English, the easier it will be to write it. But the best thing to do to improve your English writing skills is to *read.* Read as much as you can in English to learn the structure and style of the language. Rent movies based on novels. Watch the film to build your listening skills, and then read the book to improve your reading comprehension and writing skills. Good novel/movie combinations to try are those by John Grisham, including:

A Time to Kill	*The Firm*
The Client	*The Pelican Brief*

Of course, there's more to movie adaptations than legal thrillers. Here are some more good choices, from classics to contemporary, from American to world literature:

Angela's Ashes by Frank McCourt	*Gone With the Wind* by Margaret Mitchell
The Cider House Rules by John Irving	*The Joy Luck Club* by Amy Tan
The Color Purple by Alice Walker	*The Shipping News* by E. Annie Proulx
The Commitments by Roddy Doyle	*Snow Falling on Cedars* by David Guterson
The Count of Monte Cristo by Alexander Dumas	*To Kill a Mockingbird* by Harper Lee

You can also read English versions of books that you have already read in your native language. The plot and characters will already be familiar to you, so you will be able to understand more as you read.

Creating a Study Plan

Sometimes we put off work because the task just seems too big to handle. But you can make any task manageable by creating a project plan. Follow these four steps to creating a successful study plan for the TOEFL exam:

1. **Get the correct information.** Your first step is to find as much as you can about the exam. Get all the details about the TOEFL exam, including:
   - When will it be held?
   - Where will it be held?
   - How do you register?
   - When do you need to register?
   - How much does it cost?
   - What do you need to bring with you to the exam?
   - What exactly will be tested on the exam? (What subjects? What kinds of questions?)

   Some of this information has already been covered in the introduction. Chapter 6 will provide additional information. Be sure to find out answers to any questions you have about the test that are not answered in this book. (You may need to contact the TOEFL exam testing center or the university you would like to attend for those answers.)

2. **Find out what you already know and what you need to learn.** To create an effective study plan, you need to have a good sense of exactly what you need to study. Chances are you already know some of the test material well. Some of it you may only need to review. And some of it you may need to study in detail. Take a practice TOEFL exam to find out how you would do on the exam. How did you score? What do you seem to know well? What do you need to review? What do you need to study in detail?

3. **Set a time frame.** Once you have a good sense of how much studying is ahead, create a detailed study schedule. Use a calendar to set specific deadlines. If deadlines make you nervous, give yourself plenty of time for each task. Otherwise, you might have trouble keeping calm and staying on track.

   To create a good schedule, break your studying into small tasks that will get you to your learning goals. A study plan that says "Learn everything by May 1" isn't going to be helpful. However, a study plan that sets dates for learning specific material in March and April *will* enable you to learn every-thing by May 1. For example, if you need to focus on building your reading comprehension skills, you might create a schedule like the following:

Week 1	Review basic reading comprehension strategies. Start vocabulary list.
Week 2	Practice finding main idea.
Week 3	Practice vocabulary in context questions.
Week 4	Practice specific detail questions.
Week 5	Practice inference questions.
Week 6	Practice finding references.
Week 7	Take reading comprehension practice test.
Week 8	Begin reviewing grammar/usage rules. Start reading novel.
Week 9	Continue reviewing grammar/usage rules. Continue novel.

Week 10   Take structure practice test. Finish novel.

Week 11   Review writing strategies. Do practice essay.

Week 12   Do two more practice essays.

Week 13   Start overall review.

Week 14   Continue overall review.

Every day: Read several articles in an English-language newspaper.

Each week: Watch two or three TV shows and several news programs in English to build listening skills. Watch at least one movie in English.

  As you set your deadlines, think carefully about your day-to-day schedule. How much time can you spend on studying each week? Exactly when can you fit in the time to study? Be sure to be realistic about how much time you have and how much you can accomplish. Give yourself the study time you need to succeed.

Stay Away from Cramming!

BY creating a study plan, you can avoid **cramming**—trying to learn everything at the last minute. Cramming can make you very nervous, and for good reason. If you wait until a few days before the test, chances are you won't be able to learn everything. And if you stay up all night trying to get everything done, you will be too tired to study effectively.

  Create a study plan that spaces out your learning goals. Give yourself plenty of time to learn and time to review. Learn at a pace that is comfortable for you.

4. **Stick to your plan.** Make sure you have your plan written on paper and post your plan where you can see it. (Don't just keep it in your head!) Look at it regularly so you can remember what and when to study. Checking your plan regularly can also help you see how much progress you have made along the way.

  It's very important that you *don't give up* if you fall behind. Unexpected events may interrupt your plans. You may have to put in extra time at work, you may have to deal with a problem at home, or you may even come down with the flu. Or it might just take you longer to get through a task than you planned. That's okay. Stick to your schedule as much as possible, but remember that sometimes, "life gets in the way."

  For example, if you have a family problem that's keeping you from concentrating, you may need to postpone your studies to take care of that problem. And that's okay—as long as you reschedule your study time. Better to study later when you can concentrate than to waste time "studying" when you are unable to focus.

  So, if you miss one of your deadlines, don't despair. Instead, just pick up where you left off. Try to squeeze in a little extra time in the next few weeks to catch up. If that doesn't seem possible, simply adjust your schedule. Change your deadlines so that they are more realistic. Just be sure you still have enough time to finish everything before the exam.

Trouble Getting Started?

SOMETIMES it's just plain hard to get started on a big project. If you are having trouble getting going, start with an easy task, such as creating flash cards for review. That way, you will be able to accomplish something quickly and easily. And that will motivate you to move on to harder tasks.

Or, try starting your study session by reviewing or copying your notes from last session. This way, you will better remember what you have already learned while you ease into study mode.

How Do You Know What You Know?

One of the keys to successful studying is knowing what you know, and knowing what you don't know. Practice tests are one good way to measure this. But there are other ways.

One of the best ways to measure how well you know something is how well you can explain it to someone else. If you *really* know the material, you should be able to help someone else understand it. Use your learning style to explain it. For example, if you are an auditory learner, talk it out. If you are a visual learner, create diagrams and tables to demonstrate your knowledge. Rewrite your notes or make up your own quizzes with questions and answers like those on the exam. Provide an explanation along with the correct answer.

How do you know what you *don't* know? If you feel uncertain or uncomfortable during a practice test or when you try to explain it to someone else, you probably need to study more. Write down all of your questions and uncertainties. If you write down what you don't know, you can focus on searching for answers. When you get the answers, you can write them out next to the question and review them periodically. And notice how many questions you answer along the way—you will be able to see yourself making steady progress.

If you are avoiding certain topics, it's a good sign that you don't know those topics well enough for the exam. Make up your mind to tackle these areas at your next study session. Don't procrastinate!

▶ Part II: Learning Strategies

How successful you are at studying usually has less to do with how much you know and how much you study than with *how* you study. That's because some study techniques are much more effective than others. You can spend hours and hours doing practice tests, but if you don't carefully review your answers, much of your time will be wasted. You need to learn from your mistakes and study what you don't know. The best method is to use several of the following proven study techniques. They can help you make the most of your learning style and store information in your long-term memory.

Asking Questions

Asking questions is a powerful study strategy because it forces you to get actively involved in the material you want to learn. That, in turn, will help you better understand and remember the material. And there's another important benefit—asking and answering your own questions will help you be comfortable with the format of the exam.

For example, when you are reading something in English, you can ask yourself questions like those you would see on the TOEFL exam, such as:

1. What is this passage about?
2. What is the main idea?
3. What is the author's purpose?
4. What is the meaning of this word as it is used in the sentence?
5. What does "it" refer to in this passage?
6. Is this sentence a main idea or a detail?

Similarly, imagine you are on the subway. You hear two people talking about their jobs. Listen carefully to what they are saying. Then ask yourself the kinds of questions you might be asked about their conversation, such as:

1. Why is the man upset?
2. What does the man do at work?
3. What is his supervisor's name?
4. When was his last vacation?
5. What does the lady mean by "grin and bear it"?

Of course, you may not be able to answer all of your questions right away. You may need to do some extra work to find the answer.

Highlighting and Underlining

Here's a good habit to get into: Whenever you read books that belong to you, have a pen, pencil, or highlighter in your hand. That way, as you read, you can mark the words and ideas that are most important to learn or remember. Highlighting and underlining help make key ideas stand out. Important information is then easy to find when you need to take notes or review.

The key to effective highlighting or underlining is *to be selective*. Don't highlight or underline everything. If you highlight every other sentence, nothing will stand out for you on the page. Highlight only the key words and ideas.

But how do you know what you should highlight or underline? As you study for the TOEFL exam, you should highlight or underline:

- words that are defined in the text
- main ideas
- key details that support or explain main ideas
- words, grammar rules, and other items that you need to remember
- ideas or concepts that are new to you
- vocabulary words and idiomatic expressions that you are unsure about

Taking Notes

Taking notes is a terrific study strategy. It helps you understand, organize, and remember information. The secret to taking good notes is knowing what it is you should write down. As with highlighting, the key is to be selective. Take notes about the same things you would underline, especially main ideas, rules, and other items you need to learn.

Whenever possible, include examples so that you can *see* the concept clearly. For example:

Rule: Don't use *the* in front of **noncount nouns** (such as bread, wood, Spanish, peace, learning). They refer to the *general* thing, not a specific item or example.

Examples:
- *Please buy bread when you go to the store.*
- (But: *The bread he bought was moldy.* Here it's a specific bread being referred to.)
- *We wish for peace.*
- (But: *The peace did not last long.* Here a specific period of peace is referred to.)
- *Spanish is my native language.*

Making Notes

Making notes is often as important as *taking* notes. Making notes means that you *respond* to what you read. There are several ways you can respond ("talk back to") the text:

- *Write questions.* If you come across something you don't understand, write a question. *What does this mean? Why is this word used this way? Why is this the best title?* Then answer all of your questions. Here is an example. Notice how the student hears a word used in an unfamiliar way, asks a question, and then provides a detailed answer for herself to study:

    Q: Doesn't *flat* mean *smooth, without bumps or curves?* Why did the lady in the café say that her Coke was flat?

    A: The word *flat* has several meanings.

MEANING	EXAMPLE
horizontal, level	The prairie is flat.
spread out, lying at full length	He fell flat on his face.
smooth and even	The stone was flat.
absolute, unqualified	She was flat broke.
dull, monotonous	The story was flat.
(regarding carbonated beverages) having lost its effervescence (bubbles)	The Coke was flat.
(in music) below the correct pitch	Her singing is flat.
deflated	The tire was flat from running over a nail.

- *Make connections.* Any time you make connections between ideas, you improve your chances of remembering that material. For example, if Spanish is your native language, you might make the following connection:

  dormir = to sleep in Spanish

  dormitory = room with beds for students to sleep

- *Write your reactions.* Your reactions work much like connections, and they can help you remember information. For example, if you read "It's raining cats and dogs out there!" you might write:

  What an odd expression! Funny image. Easy to remember.

Outlining and Mapping Information

Outlines are great tools, especially for sequential learners. They help you focus on what's most important by making it easier to review key ideas and see relationships among those ideas. With an outline, you can see how supporting information is related to main ideas.

The basic outline structure is this:

I. Topic
    1. Main idea
        a. major supporting idea
            i. minor supporting idea

Outlines can have many layers and variations, but this is the general form. Here's an example: Verb + *up* and *out*

I. Make up
    1. to determine
        a. example: I made up my mind to pass the exam.
    2. to invent
        a. example: He made up a good excuse.
    3. to compensate, repay
        a. example: She will make up for her mistake by doing extra work.

II.   Make out
    1.   to see clearly
        a.   I can barely make out what this says.
    2.   to fare (get through or do something)
        a.   How did you make out during the interview?
    3.   *slang:* to French kiss
        a.   The teenagers made out during the whole movie.

Mapping information is similar to making an outline. The difference is that maps are less structured. You don't have to organize ideas from top to bottom. Instead, with a map, the ideas can go all over the page. The key is that you still show how the ideas are related. Here's the same example in a map instead of an outline:

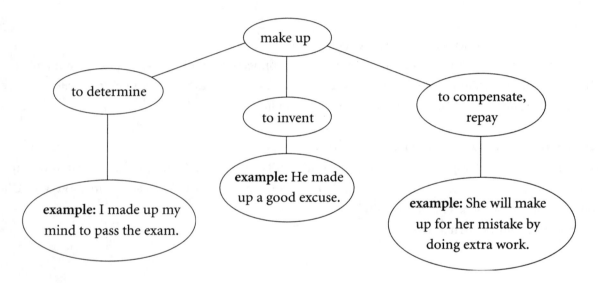

Making Flashcards

Flashcards are a simple but very effective study tool. First, buy or cut out small pieces of paper (3x5 index cards work well). On one side, put a question or word you need to learn. On the back, put the answer. You can use different colors and pictures, especially if you are a visual learner.

For example, if you are studying the past tense and participles of transitive and intransitive verbs, you could make flash cards like the following:

FRONT OF CARD

raise

BACK OF CARD

past tense:	raised
participle:	raised

FRONT OF CARD

rise

BACK OF CARD

past tense:	rose
participle:	risen

FRONT OF CARD

lay

BACK OF CARD

past tense:	laid
participle:	laid

FRONT OF CARD

lie

BACK OF CARD

past tense:	lay
participle:	lain

Memorizing versus Remembering

Imagine that you need to memorize a list of irregular verbs for the TOEFL exam. You go over and over the list until you are sure you know them. Then you take a practice test. Suddenly, you can't seem to remember the list. The verbs are used in context (within sentences), and they are not in the order you memorized. You fail the practice test.

What happened? The problem is not that you didn't study. The problem is that you didn't study wisely. You focused on *memorizing*, not *remembering*. You didn't learn the words *in context*. You didn't *use* the verbs or *practice* them by writing sample sentences. That's why, on the test, you couldn't remember them.

It's true that "repetition is the key to mastery." Try repeating a new phone number over and over, for example. Eventually you will remember it. But it may only stay in your **short-term** memory. In a few days (or maybe even a few hours), you are likely to forget the number. You need to *use it* to really learn it and store the information in your **long-term** memory. While there are some tricks you can use to help remember things in the short term, your best bet is to *use* what you are learning as much as possible and as soon as possible. For example, you can use new vocabulary words or idioms in your conversations throughout the day. You can also teach the new word or idiom to others. Here are some general strategies to help you remember information as you prepare for the TOEFL exam.

- **Learn information in small chunks.** Our brains process small chunks of information better than large ones. If you have a list of 20 vocabulary words, break that list into four lists of five words each.

- **Spread out your memory work.** Don't try to remember too much at one time. For example, if you break up those 20 words into four lists, don't try to do all four lists, one after another. Instead, try studying one list each day in several short, spaced-out sessions. For example, spend 20 minutes in the morning getting familiar with the new words. Review the words again for 15 minutes at lunchtime. Take another 15 minutes while you are waiting at the bus stop on your way home. Add another 10-minute review before bed. This kind of **distributed practice** is very effective. It's also a sneaky way to add more study time to your schedule. And, it provides lots of repetition without tiring your brain.

- **Make connections.** You learn best when you make connections to things you already know. (See "Make Connections" on page 11.)

- **Use visual aids,** especially if you are a visual learner. Help yourself "see" in your mind what you need to learn. For example, if you are learning the meaning of the expression *it's raining cats and dogs,* you can imagine cats and dogs actually raining down from the sky. This will help you remember what the expression means.

- **Use your voice,** especially if you are an auditory learner. Say aloud what you need to learn; you can even sing it if you like, especially if you can make a rhyme (for example, "speak, spoke, spoken; break, broke, broken"). Any time you are learning grammar and structure, say a sample sentence aloud several times. Try different variations, too. For example, if you are trying to memorize the irregular past tense of verbs like *wear* and *tear,* you can say a sentence like:

   My dress has a tear. It's torn.
   Her dress has a tear, too. It's also torn.

   Thinking of the sentence helps; *hearing* it aloud helps even more. And if you also *write it down,* you take an extra step toward sealing the material in your memory.

- **Use *mnemonics.*** Mnemonics are tricks to help you remember information. The most common trick is to create an *acronym.* Say you need to remember a list of words. Take the first letter from each word, then make a word from those letters. For example, imagine you are trying to memorize the following list of helping verbs:

   <u>i</u>s/was
   <u>a</u>re/were
   <u>h</u>as/have/had
   <u>c</u>an/could
   <u>w</u>ill/would
   <u>s</u>hall/should
   <u>b</u>e/been
   <u>m</u>ay/most

   You might make up the following acronyms: SWIM and BACH (the composer).

   Another trick is to make a sentence using those same letters. Using the first letter from each of the words in the helping verb list, you could write:

I am hungry. Can we share more bread?

Of course, the sillier the better (the easier to remember). So you might try something crazy, like:
I ate Hannah's car while she mashed bananas.

There are all kinds of other mnemonic tricks you can make up on your own. For example, to distinguish between the homonyms *where* and *wear,* you might remember the sentence:
You wear an earring in your ear.

If you remember that "wear" includes the word "ear," you can remember which meaning goes with which word.

Sleep on It

A rested and relaxed brain learns information best. Whenever possible, study right before you go to sleep or first thing after you wake. Try not to do anything else in between. If you study for an hour and then watch TV for an hour before bed, you won't remember as much as if you studied for an hour and then went right to bed. Right before and after sleep, you are usually in your most relaxed state—and that makes it easier for you to learn.

▶ Part III: Test-Taking Strategies

Knowing the material you will be tested on improves your chances of succeeding. But it doesn't guarantee that you will do your best on the test. The TOEFL exam doesn't just test your knowledge of the English language. Like all standardized tests, it also measures your test-taking skills. In this section, you will learn strategies for taking standardized tests like the TOEFL exam.

Learn about the Test

One sure way to increase your chances of test success is to find out as much as you can about the exam. If you don't know what to expect on the test, you won't know how to study. It is likely that you will be extra anxious about the exam, too. The more you know about the test you are going to take, the better you can prepare—and the more relaxed you will be when the test comes.

You already know what kind of test the TOEFL exam is. You know that there are four sections: Listening Comprehension, Structure and Written Expression, Reading Comprehension, and Writing. You know that the test questions for the first three sections are all multiple-choice. You know how much time you have to complete each section. But until you look at actual sample questions, you still don't *really* know what to expect. For example, in the Listening Comprehension section, what kind of passages will you listen to? What kind of questions will you be asked about those passages?

Getting sample tests and working with skill builders like this book can help you in many ways. You will get used to the kind of questions you will be asked and the level of difficulty of those questions. You will also become familiar with the format and comfortable with the length of the exam.

Handling Test Stress

Test anxiety is like the common cold. Most people suffer from it periodically. It won't kill you, but it can make your life miserable for several days.

Like a cold, test anxiety can be mild or severe. You may just feel an underlying nervousness about the upcoming exam. Or you may be nearly paralyzed with worry, especially if there's a lot riding on the exam. Whatever the case, if you have test anxiety, you need to deal with it. Fortunately, there are many strategies to help prevent and treat test anxiety.

PREVENTION

The best "cure" for test anxiety is to *prevent* it from happening in the first place. Test anxiety is often caused by a lack of preparation. If you learn all you can about the test and create and follow a study plan, you should be in good shape when it comes to exam time. Here are some other, more general strategies:

- **Establish and stick to a routine.** Routines help us feel more comfortable and in control. Whenever possible, study at the same time and in the same place. Make your test preparation a habit that's hard to break. Studying for the TOEFL exam will become easier as it becomes routine. You will be more likely to avoid distractions, and others will know not to disturb you during your TOEFL exam time. Set routines for other aspects of your life, too, such as exercise and paying the bills.
- **Keep your general stress level low.** If there are a lot of other stresses in your life, chances are a big test will make those other stresses seem more difficult to manage. Remember to keep things in perspective. If something is beyond your control, don't waste your energy worrying about it. Instead, think of how you can handle what *is* in your control.
- **Stay confident.** Remind yourself that you are smart and capable. You can take this test—and you can do well on it. Remember, you know more today than you did yesterday.
- **Stay healthy.** When your body is run down or ill, your brainpower will suffer, too. And you are much more likely to be overtaken by worries. Take care of yourself throughout the test preparation process. (See more information on page 18.)

TREATMENT

If it's too late to prevent test anxiety, don't panic. You can still treat it effectively. Here are some strategies to help reduce test stress:

- **Face your fears.** Admit that you are worried about the test and examine the reasons why. Your fears won't change the fact that you have to take the test, but they can paralyze you and keep you from studying and doing well on the exam. Acknowledge your fears, put them in perspective, and refuse to let your fears hurt you.

One very helpful strategy is to write your fears down. When you put your worries on paper, they often seem more manageable than when they are bouncing around in your brain and keeping you up at night. Once you write down your fears, you can then brainstorm solutions. For example, imagine you are worried about not being able to find enough time to get your work done and finish studying. Once you put this fear down on paper, you can begin to figure out how to squeeze in the hours you will need to get everything done. And you will feel more in control.

- **Keep things in perspective.** Yes, the TOEFL exam is a big deal; it's an important test. But even if you do poorly on the test, is it the end of the world? Will your family stop loving you? Will you be less of a person? Of course not. Perspective is very important to performance. Of course you should be serious about succeeding. But don't lose sight of other important aspects of your life.

- **Be sufficiently prepared.** Anxiety often comes from feeling insecure in a new situation. But if you prepare well, using this and other books, the TOEFL exam will not be new to you. And if you follow your study plan, you will know how to answer the questions you will face on the exam. If you have fallen behind, remember that it's not too late to catch up.

- **Stop making excuses.** Excuses may give you some comfort in the short term, but they don't take away test anxiety—and they won't help you do well on the exam. In fact, excuses often make things worse by making you feel guilty and powerless. Don't let yourself feel like a victim. You may have a lot of things going on in your life and many things may interfere with your studies. But you have the power to choose how you deal with your circumstances.

- **Imagine yourself succeeding.** Highly successful people will often tell you that one of their secrets is **visualization.** In their mind's eye, they *see* themselves succeeding. They imagine the situations they will face, and they imagine themselves handling those situations beautifully.

Visualization is a very powerful tool. It's a way of telling yourself that *you believe you can do it.* The power of this kind of belief is staggering. If you believe you can accomplish something, you are far more likely to accomplish it. Likewise, if you believe you *can't* do something, you are far more likely to *fail* to achieve that goal. Positive visualization will make it easier for you to study and manage your entire test preparation process.

Anyone can use the power of visualization. Picture yourself sitting calmly through the exam, answering one question after another correctly. See yourself getting excellent test results in the mail. Imagine yourself telling family and friends how well you did on the exam. Picture yourself receiving the college acceptance letter or job offer you desire.

- **Stick to your study plan.** Test anxiety can paralyze you if you let it. And before you know it, you have missed several deadlines on your study plan. Guess what? That will only make your test anxiety worse. As soon as you feel your stomach start to flutter with test anxiety, go back to your study plan. Make an extra effort to stick to your schedule.

Be Healthy

It's difficult to do your best on a test when you are not feeling well. Your mind *and* body need to be in good shape for the test. If you let your body get run down, you may become ill. That, in turn, will set you back on your study schedule. And that may lead to test anxiety, which can make you feel run down again. This is a downward spiral you need to avoid. If you do feel run down, take a day or two to rest and feel better. Maybe you will be two days behind your study schedule, but when you continue, your studying will be more effective. As long as it's not a constant problem for you and as long as you are not using illness to avoid studying, you will do yourself a favor by resting.

Take good care of yourself throughout the entire test preparation process and especially in the week before the exam. Here are some specific suggestions for staying healthy:

1. **Get enough rest.** Some of us need eight or more hours of sleep each night. Others are happy with just five or six. You know what your body needs for you to feel clear-headed and energized. Make sleep a priority so that you are able to concentrate the day of the exam. If you have trouble sleeping, try one of the following strategies:
   - Get exercise during the day. A tired body will demand more sleep.
   - Get up and study. If you study in the night when you can't sleep, you can cut out study time from the next day so you can take a nap or get to bed earlier. (Of course, sometimes studying will help you fall asleep in the first place.)
   - Relax with a hot bath, a good book (in English), or sleep-inducing foods. A glass of warm milk, for example, may help you fall back asleep.
   - Do some gentle stretching or seated forward bends. Try to touch your toes with your legs outstretched. This is a relaxing posture. Or, practice a few relaxation poses from yoga: child's pose, corpse pose, or cat stretch (see a good website like www.yoga.com for details).
   - Spend a few minutes doing deep breathing. Fill your lungs slowly and completely. Hold for a few seconds and then release slowly and completely. You can practice deep breathing any time you need to relax or regain focus.
   - Write down your worries. Again, putting your fears on paper can help make them more manageable.

2. **Eat well.** Keeping a healthy diet is often as hard as getting enough rest when you are busy preparing for a test. But how you eat can have a tremendous impact on how you study and how you perform on the exam. You may think you are saving time by eating fast food instead of cooking a healthy meal. But in reality, you are depriving your body of the nutrition it needs to be at its best. You may think that a couple extra cups of coffee a day are a good thing because you can stay up later and study. But in reality, you are "tricking" your brain into thinking that it's awake and making yourself more dependent on caffeine.

Foods to avoid—especially at test-time—include high-sugar, high-calorie, low-nutrition foods, such as donuts, chips, and cookies. Instead, find healthy substitutes such as the following:

INSTEAD OF . . .	EAT . . .
donuts	low-sugar, multi-grain cereal
chips	carrot sticks
cookies	natural granola bar
ice cream	low-fat yogurt
sugary soda	fresh squeezed fruit juice
giant-sized coffee	green tea

3. **Get exercise.** You hardly have the time to study, so how can you find the time to exercise? As difficult as it may be, it's important to squeeze exercise into your busy schedule. Even light exercise, such as a brisk walk to the store, can dramatically improve your brainpower. For one thing, exercising can help you clear your head, especially if you are preoccupied with many things and need to get focused on your work. For another, if you exercise, you will have more energy during the day and sleep better at night. That means all of your study time will be more productive. In addition, your exercise time can actually double as study time. For example, you can review material while you are riding an exercise bike. You can go through verb conjugations while you are race-walking around the park. If you exercise with a partner, you can practice your English speaking and listening skills. You can watch TV in English while you run on the treadmill. And here's another bonus: exercise helps relieve stress. So especially if you are dealing with test anxiety, make exercise a priority.

Multiple-Choice Test Strategies

Multiple-choice is the most popular question format for standardized tests like the TOEFL exam. Understandably so: Multiple-choice questions are easy and fast to grade. They are also popular because they are generally considered *objective*. They are questions based solely on information and don't allow the test taker to express opinions.

Multiple-choice questions have three parts:

Stem: the question
Options: the answer choices
Distracters: the incorrect answers

Stem: By "It's raining cats and dogs," the man probably means
Options:
a) It's been a long time since it rained.
b) It is raining heavily.
c) He needs an umbrella.
d) His pets are out of control.

In this question, the correct answer is **b**. The other options are all distracters. Here are some strategies to help you answer multiple-choice questions correctly:

1. **Circle or underline key words in the stem.** These are the words that help you search for the correct answer. For example, in the stem:

   The modern bicycle has all of the following safety features except

   the key words are "modern," "safety features" and "except." You need to look in the passage for the safety features of modern bicycles. And you need to find the answer that is *not* specifically mentioned in the passage.

2. **Immediately cross out all answers you know are incorrect.** This will help you find the correct answer. It is an especially important step if you have to guess at the answer.

3. **Beware of distracter techniques.** Test developers will often put in look-alike options, easily confused options, and silly options. For example, in the "raining cats and dogs" example, choice **c** may be true according to the passage, but it doesn't give the meaning of the idiom as asked in the stem. Therefore it is the wrong choice. Choice **d** is the silliest option and is the one you should probably eliminate first. Even if you don't know the meaning of the idiom, you should have realized that it *is* an idiom and that the cats and dogs are not real; it is a figure of speech. Still, if you did choose this option, don't despair. Just read more carefully next time and be aware that some choices can be tricky.

4. **Read stems carefully** to be sure you understand *exactly* what is being asked. Watch for tricky wording such as "All of the following are true *except*." You will find distracters that are accurate and may sound right but do not apply to that stem. For example, if you don't notice the "except" on the bicycle question stem, you might choose a distracter that *is* a safety feature of the modern bicycle. The answer would be accurate but wrong because you did not read the question carefully.

5. **Beware of absolutes.** Read carefully any stem that includes words like *always, never, none* or *all.* An answer may sound perfectly correct and the general principal may be correct. However, it may not be true in all circumstances.

Almost There: Strategies for the Final Days Before the Exam

Your months of preparation will soon pay off. You have worked hard, and the test is just a week or two away. Here are some tips for making sure things go smoothly in the home stretch.

The week before the test:

- Be sure you know exactly where you are taking the test. Get detailed directions. Take a practice drive so you know exactly how long it will take you to get there.
- Review everything you have learned.
- Get quality sleep each night.
- Practice visualization—see yourself performing well on the TOEFL exam.

Should You Guess?

IF you aren't sure about the answer to a multiple-choice question, should you guess? In most cases, yes. The general rule of thumb is this:

Guess if you can eliminate at least one answer. Multiple-choice questions usually have four or five options, only one of which is right. That gives you a 20–25% chance of guessing correctly. If you have four options and eliminate one distracter, that increases your chances to 33%. If you eliminate two distracters, you have a 50/50 chance of getting the right answer. Those odds are worth taking a risk, even if you receive a slight penalty for an incorrect answer.

On the computer-based TOEFL exam, your score will be lowered by random guessing. Only guess if you have eliminated *at least* one distracter.

On the supplemental paper-based TOEFL exam, however, you should guess *even if you can't eliminate one or more distracters.* On the paper test, your score is based on the number of questions you answer correctly. There is no penalty for answering a question incorrectly.

The day before the test:

- Get to bed early.
- Get light exercise. Don't work out too hard. You don't want to be sore or physically exhausted the day of the exam.
- Get everything you will need ready: pencils/pens, admission materials/documentation, any mints or snacks you'd like to have along.
- Make a list of everything you need to bring so you don't forget anything in the morning.

The day of the test:

- Get up early. Make sure you set your alarm. Ask a family member or friend to make sure you are up on time.
- Eat a light, healthy breakfast, such as yogurt and granola or a low-fat, low-sugar cereal and fruit.
- Dress comfortably. Wear layers so that you can take off a shirt or sweater if you are too warm in the test room.
- Don't drastically alter your diet. For example, if you drink coffee every morning, don't skip it—you could get a headache. However, don't go for that second cup or super-sized portion. Too much caffeine can make you jittery during the exam, and you can "crash" when the caffeine wears off.

At the test site:

- Chat with others, but *not* about the test. That might only make you more nervous.
- Think positive. Remember, you are prepared.

- Avoid squeezing in a last-minute review. Instead, visualize your success and plan your reward for after the test is over.
- Make sure you read and understand all test directions clearly. How should you fill out the answer sheet? What if you want to change an answer? Can you write on the test booklet? What is the time limit? What if you have technical difficulties during the exam? Don't hesitate to ask questions about *anything* that is unclear.

After the test:
- Celebrate!

2 ▶ Reading Comprehension Skills

Strong reading comprehension skills are essential for success on the TOEFL exam and throughout your college career. In this chapter, you will learn exactly what the reading comprehension section of the TOEFL exam is like. You will also review and practice basic reading comprehension skills so you can better understand what you read and do well on the exam.

AS A COLLEGE student, you will spend a great deal of time reading. And because you will attend an American university, the textbooks, articles, lecture notes, and websites you read for class will be in English. Obviously, you will need to understand what you read to do well in your classes. That's why Section 3 of the TOEFL exam is devoted to reading comprehension skills; admissions officers want to be sure you will be able to understand all of your reading assignments.

▶ TOEFL Exam Reading Comprehension: What to Expect

In many ways, the TOEFL exam reading comprehension section is much like reading comprehension sections on other standardized tests. You will be asked to read a short passage (usually no more than five to seven paragraphs). Then you will be asked to answer several multiple-choice questions about that passage.

Reading passages on the TOEFL exam are typically factual and often academic in nature. The passages are, in fact, quite similar to the kind of texts you will read in the college classroom. For example, you might read about the history of the French Revolution, the conventions of Greek tragedies, the cellular structure of plants, or the trickle-down theory of economics. TOEFL exam reading passages are usually one to five paragraphs long, though a few may run as long as seven or eight.

Computer-Based Test vs. Paper-Based Test

THERE are a few differences between the new computer-based TOEFL and the old paper-based exam. Most of those differences have to do with formatting (such as the number of questions), not the content. The type and difficulty of the passages and questions remain the same.

The chart below compares the reading comprehension sections on the two tests:

Computer-Based TOEFL exam	Supplemental Paper-Based TOEFL exam
70–90 minutes.	55 minutes.
44–55 questions.	50 questions.
3–6 reading passages.	5 reading passages.
6–10 questions per passage.	Average of 10 questions per passage.
Questions may include pictures that refer to the passage.	Questions do not include pictures.
Questions may have two correct answers.	Questions have only one correct answer.

Source: *Barron's Passkey to the TOEFL,* 4th ed., 2001.

Kinds of Reading Comprehension Passages and Questions on the TOEFL Exam

With very few exceptions, most reading comprehension questions on the TOEFL exam will fall into one of nine categories:

- main idea
- vocabulary
- specific fact or detail
- exceptions
- location of information
- inferences
- references
- paraphrased sentences (computer-based test only)
- sentence insertion (computer-based test only)

Main Idea

These questions ask you to identify the main idea of the passage (or sometimes part of a passage, such as a specific paragraph).

Sample Questions:

- The main idea of this passage is best expressed in which sentence?
- Which of the following would be the best title for this passage?
- What is this passage mainly about?
- What is the author's main purpose in this passage?

Vocabulary

There are two types of vocabulary questions. One kind asks you to determine the meaning of a word as it is used in the passage. The other, which appears on the computer-based tests, asks you to identify a synonym for the vocabulary word.

Sample Questions:

- The word *indelible* in paragraph 3 most likely means:
- The word *protest* in paragraph 5 is closest in meaning to:
- The word *remarkable* in paragraph 2 could best be replaced by:
- Look at the word charming in the passage. [highlighted word will be pointed out in the passage] Click on another word in the **bold** text that is closest in meaning to charming .

Specific Fact or Detail

This kind of question asks you to identify a specific fact or detail mentioned in the passage.

Sample Questions:

- What causes a lunar eclipse?
- When did the last lunar eclipse occur?
- What did many pagan cultures believe caused a lunar eclipse?

Exceptions

These questions ask you to identify which item *was not* specifically mentioned in the passage.

Sample Questions:

- Which characteristic does NOT describe an endothermic reaction?
- Which of the following was NOT identified as a cause of the stock market crash?
- A person with bipolar disorder would NOT exhibit which symptom?

Location of Information

This kind of question asks you to identify the exact place in the passage where specific information is provided.

Sample Questions:

- Where in the passage does the author define the term *endothermic*?
- Click on the sentence in paragraph 2 in which the author mentions the symptoms of bipolar disorder.
- Click on the paragraph that discusses the treatments for bipolar disorder.

Inferences

This type of question asks you to make an inference (draw a logical conclusion) based on the information in the passage.

Sample Questions:
- The author suggests that insects with more than eight legs:
- This passage suggests that Greek tragedies are still so powerful because:

References

These questions ask you to determine what a specific word or phrase in the passage refers to. (The word or phrase is often a pronoun, such as "its.")

Sample Questions:
- The word *them* in paragraph 3 refers to:
- Look at the word it in the passage. Click on the word or phrase in the bold text that it refers to.

Paraphrased Sentences

This kind of question asks you to identify the sentence that best *paraphrases* (restates) one or more sentences from the passage.

Sample Questions:
- What does the author mean by the sentence the design was radically different from the other designs proposed ?
- What does the author mean by the statement Unfortunately, many people do not understand that bipolar disorder is a mental illness and that patients' mood swings are not in their control ?

Sentence Insertion

These questions ask you to identify the best (most logical) place within the passage to insert a new sentence. You will be asked to choose from several possible choices marked with a small square (■).

Sample Question:
The following sentence can be added to paragraph 2:

These cycles of mania and depression are often unpredictable and can vary greatly in length.

Where would this sentence best fit in the paragraph? Click on the square (■) to add the sentence to the paragraph.

▶ Essential Reading Comprehension Skills

Now that you have a better idea of what to expect on the reading comprehension section of the TOEFL exam, it's time to review basic reading comprehension skills. These strategies will help you better understand what you read and help you do well on the exam.

Active Reading

People often think of reading as a passive activity. After all, you are just sitting there, looking at words on a page. But reading should actually be an active exercise. When you read, you should *interact* with the text, paying careful attention and being involved as you read. Whenever you read—for the TOEFL exam, for class, for pleasure—use these active reading strategies to improve your reading comprehension:

SKIM AHEAD AND JUMP BACK

Skimming ahead helps prepare you for your reading task. Before you begin reading, scan the text to see what's ahead. Is the reading broken into sections? What are the main topics of those sections? In what order are they covered? What key words or ideas are boldfaced, bulleted, boxed, or otherwise highlighted?

When you finish reading, jump back. Review the summaries, headings, and highlighted information. (This includes what you highlighted, too.) Jumping back helps you remember the information you just read. You can see how each idea fits into the whole and how ideas and information are connected.

LOOK UP UNFAMILIAR VOCABULARY WORDS

The TOEFL exam will test your knowledge of English words. One of the best ways to build your vocabulary is to *always* look up words you don't know. You need to know what all the words in a sentence mean to fully understand what someone is saying. Remember, a key word or phrase can change the meaning of a whole passage.

So, whenever possible, have a dictionary with you when you read. Circle and look up any unfamiliar words right away. (Circling them makes them easier to find if you lose your place.) Write the meaning of the word in the margin. That way, you won't have to look up the meaning again if you forget it; it will always be there for you to refer to. If you don't own the book, write the vocabulary word and its definition in a notebook.

If you don't have a dictionary with you, try to figure out what the word means. What clues does the author provide in the sentence and surrounding sentences? Mark the page or write down the word somewhere so you can look it up later. See how closely you were able to guess its meaning. (You will learn more about how to figure out meanings on page 33.)

MARK UP THE TEXT

As you read, mark up the text (or notepaper if the text doesn't belong to you). This includes three strategies you learned in the "Study Skills" section of Chapter 1:

- highlight or underline key words and ideas
- take notes
- make notes

See pages 9–11 to review these important active reading strategies.

Careful, active reading will help you improve your overall reading comprehension skills and make reading a more pleasant experience. It will also be your best strategy for tackling the reference and paraphrased sentence questions on the TOEFL exam.

A Tip for Reference and Paraphrased Sentence Questions

SENTENCES that ask you to identify a reference or the best paraphrase for a sentence are testing a similar skill. In both cases, you need to show that you understand what a particular sentence is saying. The following strategy can help ensure that you give the correct answer.

First, eliminate any answers that you know are incorrect. Then, take the remaining choices and insert them one at a time into the sentence or paragraph. Does the answer make sense in the context of the sentence or paragraph? If not, it is not the correct answer.

For example, notice how this works with the following reference question:

The word *they* in paragraph 3 refers to:

    a. people suffering from bipolar disorder.

    b. symptoms of bipolar disorder.

    c. family members of people with bipolar disorder.

    d. people who have occasional mood swings.

Here's the sentence in which *they* is used:

    They are often greatly relieved to learn that they suffer from a treatable medical condition.

It's clear that "they" refers to people, not symptoms, so we can immediately rule out answer **b**. Now, we can begin the process of elimination by replacing "they" with each of the remaining answers:

    a. *People who suffer from bipolar disorder are often greatly relieved to learn that they suffer from a treatable medical condition.*

    c. *Family members of people with bipolar disorder are often greatly relieved to learn that they suffer from a treatable medical condition.*

    d. *People who have occasional mood swings are often greatly relieved to learn that they suffer from a treatable medical condition.*

This process makes it clear that **a** is the correct answer.

Finding the Main Idea

Standardized reading comprehension tests always have questions about the main idea of the passage. But just what is the main idea, anyway, and why is it so important?

Often, students confuse the *main idea* of a passage with its *topic*. But they are two very different things. The topic or subject of a passage is what the passage is *about*. The main idea, on the other hand, is what the writer wants to say *about* that subject. For example, take a look at the paragraph below:

The immune system uses a complex and remarkable communications network to defend the body against infection. Inside the body, millions and millions of cells are organized into sets and subsets. These cells pass information back and forth like clouds of bees swarming around a hive. The result is a sensitive system of checks and balances that produce a prompt, appropriate, and effective immune response.

The *topic* of this paragraph is "the immune system." But "the immune system" is not the main idea. The main idea is what the writer is saying *about* the immune system. Here, the main idea is expressed in the first sentence: *The immune system uses a complex and remarkable communications network to defend the body against infection.*

> **Topic/Subject:** What the passage is about.
> **Main idea:** The overall fact, feeling, or thought a writer wants to convey about his or her subject.

The main idea is so important because it is the idea that the passage *adds up to*. It's what holds all of the ideas in the passage together and is the writer's main point.

To hold all of the ideas in the passage together, main ideas need to be sufficiently **general.** That is, they need to be broad enough for all of the other sentences in the passage to fit underneath, like people underneath an umbrella. For example, look at the following choices for the main idea of the immune system paragraph:

a. The immune system has its own system of checks and balances.
b. The immune system consists of billions of cells.
c. The immune system is a very complex and effective communication system.

The only answer that can be correct is **c**, because this is the idea that the paragraph adds up to. It's what holds together all of the information in the paragraph. Choices **a** and **b** are both too specific to be the main idea. They aren't broad enough to cover all of the ideas in the passage, which discusses the number of cells, the system of checks and balances, and other information.

Of course, an idea can be *too* general to be the main idea. For example, "The immune system is what protects the body from infection" is too broad to be the main idea for the immune system paragraph we have seen. This sentence would work better as the overall main idea for a passage that covers all of the functions and aspects of the immune system, not just its communications network.

Much of the writing you will see in textbooks and on the TOEFL exam will follow a very basic pattern of **general idea ➔ specific support.** That is, the writer will state the main idea he or she wants to convey about the topic and then provide support for that idea, usually in the form of specific facts and details. This format can be diagrammed as follows:

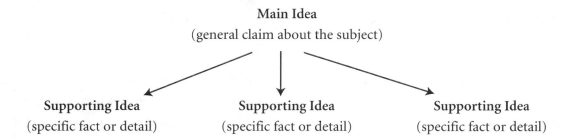

In the immune system paragraph, for example, the first sentence states the main idea—a general claim about the subject. The rest of the sentences offer specific facts and details to "prove" that the immune system is a complex and effective communication network.

DISTINGUISHING MAIN IDEAS FROM SUPPORTING IDEAS

If you're not sure whether something is a main idea or a supporting idea, ask yourself the following question: Is the sentence making a *general statement,* or is it providing *specific information*? In the paragraph below, for example, most of the sentences (except one) are too specific to be the main idea of the paragraph. Only one sentence—the first—is general enough to serve as an umbrella or net for the whole paragraph.

> Many people are afraid of snakes, but most snakes aren't as dangerous as people think they are. There are more than 2,500 different species of snakes around the world. Only a small percentage of those species are poisonous, and only a few species have venom strong enough to kill a human being. Furthermore, snakes bite only 1,000–2,000 people in the United States each year, and only ten of those bites (that's less than 1%) result in death. Statistically, many other animals are far more dangerous than snakes. In fact, in this country, more people die from dog bites each year than from snakes.

Notice how the first sentence makes a general claim about snakes (that they "aren't as dangerous as people think they are"). Then the rest of the sentences in the paragraph provide details and specific facts that support the main idea.

Writers often provide clues that can help you distinguish between main ideas and their support. Here are some of the most common words and phrases used to introduce specific examples:

for example	for instance	in particular
in addition	furthermore	some
others	specifically	such as

These signal words usually mean that a supporting fact or idea will follow. If you are having trouble finding the main idea of a paragraph, try eliminating sentences that begin with these phrases. (Did you notice that one of the sentences in the snake paragraph begins with one of these transitional words?)

TOPIC SENTENCES

Writers often state their main ideas in one or two sentences so that readers can be very clear about the main point of the passage. In a longer text, such as an essay, the main idea is often called the **thesis** or **theme**. But within a text, each *paragraph* also has its own main idea. In fact, that's the definition of a **paragraph**: *a group of sentences about the same idea.* The sentence that expresses the main idea of a paragraph is called a **topic sentence.** The first sentence in both the immune system and snake paragraphs state their main ideas. Those sentences are therefore the topic sentences for those paragraphs.

Topic sentences are often located at the beginning of paragraphs, but not always. Sometimes writers begin with specific supporting ideas and lead up to the main idea. In this case, the topic sentence would probably be at the end of the paragraph. Notice how we can rewrite the snake paragraph to put the topic sentence at the end of the passage:

> There are more than 2,500 different species of snakes around the world. Only a small percentage of those species are poisonous, and only a few species have venom strong enough to kill a human being. Snakes bite only 1,000–2,000 people in the United States each year, and only 10 of those bites (that's less than 1%) result in death. Statistically, many other animals are far more dangerous than snakes. In fact, in this country, more people die from dog bites each year than from snakes. Clearly, snakes aren't as dangerous as people think they are.

Sometimes the topic sentence is not found at the beginning or end of a paragraph but rather somewhere in the middle. Other times there isn't a clear topic sentence at all. But that doesn't mean the paragraph doesn't have a main idea. It's there, but the author has chosen not to express it in a clear topic sentence. In that case, you will have to look carefully at the paragraph for clues about the main idea.

Just as the sentences within a paragraph support the main idea of that paragraph, the main idea of *each paragraph* supports the main idea of the entire passage. Most questions about main idea on the TOEFL exam will probably ask you to identify the overall main idea. Writers often state their overall main idea, but these thesis statements are not quite as common as topic sentences in paragraphs. You will often have to look carefully at the answer options and decide which of those ideas best encompasses all of the ideas in the passage.

Practice 1

Read the passage below carefully. After you read, answer the questions that follow. Keep in mind that you will be asked to identify not only the overall main idea but also the main idea of individual paragraphs. [Answers and explanations to all practice questions are located in Appendix A.]

Bicycles

(1)Today, bicycles are so common that it's hard to believe they haven't always been around. (2)But two hundred years ago, bicycles didn't even exist, and the first bicycle, invented in Germany in 1818, was nothing like our bicycles today. (3)It was made of wood and didn't even have pedals. (4)Since then, however, numerous innovations and improvements in design have made the bicycle one of the most popular means of recreation and transportation around the world.

(5)In 1839, Kirkpatrick Macmillan, a Scottish blacksmith, dramatically improved upon the original bicycle design. (6)Macmillan's machine had tires with iron rims to keep them from getting worn down. (7)He also used foot-operated cranks similar to pedals so his bicycle could be ridden at a quick pace. (8)It didn't look much like a modern bicycle, though, because its back wheel was substantially larger than its front wheel. (9)In 1861, the French Michaux brothers took the evolution of the bicycle a step further by inventing an improved crank mechanism.

(10)Ten years later, James Starley, an English inventor, revolutionized bicycle design. (11)He made the front wheel many times larger than the back wheel, put a gear on the pedals to make the bicycle more efficient, and lightened the wheels by using wire spokes. (12)Although this bicycle was much lighter and less tiring to ride, it was still clumsy, extremely top-heavy, and ridden mostly for entertainment.

(13)It wasn't until 1874 that the first truly modern bicycle appeared on the scene. (14)Invented by another Englishman, H.J. Lawson, the "safety bicycle" would look familiar to today's cyclists. (15)This bicycle had equal sized wheels, which made it less prone to toppling over. (16)Lawson also attached a chain to the pedals to drive the rear wheel. (17)With these improvements, the bicycle became extremely popular and useful for transportation. (18)Today they are built, used, and enjoyed all over the world.

1. What is the *subject* of this passage?
   a. kinds of bicycles
   b. the history of bicycles
   c. how to ride a bicycle
   d. bicycle safety

2. The main idea of this passage is best expressed in which sentence?

   a. Sentence (1): Today, bicycles are so common that it's hard to believe they haven't always been around.

   b. Sentence (13): It wasn't until 1874 that the first truly modern bicycle appeared on the scene.

   c. Sentence (4): Since then, however, numerous innovations and improvements in design have made the bicycle one of the most popular means of recreation and transportation around the world.

   d. Sentence (18): Today they are built, used, and enjoyed all over the world.

3. Which of the following would be the best title for this passage?

   a. Bicycles are Better

   b. A Ride through the History of Bicycles

   c. Cycle Your Way to Fitness

   d. The Popularity of Bicycles

4. Which sentence best expresses the main idea of paragraph 2?

   a. Macmillan was a great inventor.

   b. Macmillan's bike didn't look much like our modern bikes.

   c. Macmillan's bike could be ridden quickly.

   d. Macmillan made important changes in bicycle design.

5. What is the author's main purpose in paragraph 4?

   a. To show how Lawson's improvements made bicycles popular.

   b. To show how innovative Lawson's design was.

   c. To show how dramatically bicycle designs have changed.

   d. To show why bicycles are so popular today.

Determining Meaning from Context

Of course, during the TOEFL exam, you won't be allowed to use a dictionary. So how will you figure out what unfamiliar words mean? And how can you fully understand what you are reading if you don't know all the words?

Fortunately, by looking carefully at **context**—the sentences and ideas surrounding an unfamiliar word—you can often figure out exactly what that word means. The vocabulary questions in the reading comprehension section of the TOEFL exam do test your knowledge of English vocabulary—if you know the word in question, you often don't even need to consider the context. But vocabulary questions are also designed to test your ability to use context to determine meaning. That's because this is an essential reading comprehension skill. Even if you are completely fluent in English, you will come across unfamiliar vocabulary words in your reading. And familiar words may have meanings with which you are not familiar. You will need context to figure out what those words mean in those situations.

So let's look at an example to see how you can use context to determine meaning. Read the sentences below carefully and actively.

By the end of the day, I was *famished*. I'd skipped breakfast and had only eaten a pear for lunch.

What does *famished* mean?
  a. famous
  b. very tired
  c. very hungry
  d. impatient

The context here clearly suggests answer **c,** *very hungry.* The second sentence tells us that the speaker had no breakfast and very little lunch. It's safe to conclude, then, that *famished* has something to do with eating (or rather, *not* eating). *Famous* may *sound* like *famished,* but nothing in the passage suggests that *famished* has anything to do with being famous—or with being tired or impatient, either.

When you come across unfamiliar words, then, your job as a reader is to look for context clues that can help you determine what that word means. Here's another example:

I am so angry! The autographed picture of Michael Jordan turned out to be *bogus.* The man who sold it to me had signed it himself!

Bogus most nearly means
  a. fake, false
  b. believable
  c. interesting
  d. expensive

Here, the second sentence gives us the clue we need to figure out what *bogus* means. Because the man who sold the picture "signed it himself," we know that it's not really Michael Jordan's autograph on the picture. Therefore, the autograph is a fake, and **a** is the best answer. It may also have been expensive, but there are no context clues to suggest that meaning.

Tips for Vocabulary Questions

When you're trying to determine meaning from context on an exam, two strategies can help you find the best answer:

1. First, use the context to determine whether the vocabulary word is something **positive or negative.** If the word seems like something positive, then eliminate the options that are negative, and vice versa. For example, you can tell from the context that *bogus* is something negative; otherwise, the speaker wouldn't be "so angry." We can therefore eliminate choices **b** and **c.**

2. Second, **replace the vocabulary word** with the remaining answers, one at a time. Does the answer make sense when you read the sentence? If not, you can eliminate that answer. In the *bogus* example, we are left with two options: choice **a**, *fake, false* and choice **d**, *expensive*. Either situation might make the speaker angry, so we must look to see which word makes sense with the context of the third sentence. That sentence, of course, tells us that the autograph isn't real, so choice **a** is the only possible correct option.

Practice 2

[Answers and explanations to all practice questions are located in Appendix A.]

1. He was so nervous that his voice was *quavering*.
   a. thundering, booming confidently
   b. trembling, shaking noticeably
   c. quiet, whispering softly
   d. making a quacking sound

2. I accidentally told Nell about her surprise birthday party. What a stupid *blunder!* A *blunder* is
   a. a person who can't keep secrets.
   b. an idea.
   c. a mistake.
   d. a get-together.

   Questions 3 and 4 refer to the paragraph below.

   The Sami are an indigenous people living in the northern parts of Norway, Sweden, Finland, and Russia's Kola peninsula. Originally, the Sami religion was <u>animistic</u>; that is, for them, nature and natural objects had a conscious life, a spirit. One was expected to move quietly in the wilderness to avoid <u>disturbing</u> the woodland spirits. The great conqueror Ghengis Khan is said to have declared that the Sami were one people he would never try to fight against. Since the Sami were not warriors and did not believe in war, they simply disappeared in times of conflict. They were known as "peaceful retreaters."

3. The word *animistic* as it is used in sentence 2 most nearly means
   a. the irrational belief in supernatural beings.
   b. the belief that animals and plants have souls.
   c. the belief that animals are gods.
   d. the primitive belief that people are reincarnated as animals.

4. The word *disturbing* in sentence 3 could best be replaced by which word?
   a. angering
   b. hurting
   c. bothering
   d. pleasing

Identifying Specific Facts and Details

On standardized tests, you will often be asked to identify specific facts and details from what you read. The TOEFL exam will ask you to do this in three different ways:

1. By identifying a specific fact or detail mentioned in the passage.
2. By identifying information that was *not* specifically mentioned in the passage.
3. By identifying the place in the passage where specific information can be found.

Of course, you can't be expected to remember every detail. So how do you identify specific facts and details quickly and accurately, especially when a passage is several paragraphs long?

The idea behind these questions isn't for you to *memorize* everything in the passage. Rather, these questions test (1) how carefully you read and (2) your ability to know where to look for specific information within a passage. For example, take another look at the snakes paragraph:

> Many people are afraid of snakes, but most snakes aren't as dangerous as people think they are. There are more than 2,500 different species of snakes around the world. Only a small percentage of those species are poisonous, and only a few species have venom strong enough to kill a human being. Furthermore, snakes bite only 1,000–2,000 people in the United States each year, and only ten of those bites (that's less than 1%) result in death. Statistically, many other animals are far more dangerous than snakes. In fact, in this country, more people die from dog bites each year than from snakes.

On the TOEFL exam, you might be asked a question like the following:

How many species of snakes are there worldwide?
   a. between 1,000–2,000
   b. less than 100
   c. less than 2,500
   d. more than 2,500

There are several numbers in this passage, and if you didn't read carefully, you could easily choose the wrong answer. The correct answer is **d**, more than 2,500. This fact is clearly stated in the second sentence.

The best way to find this information is to **use the key words from the question** as your guide. In this example, the key words are *how many* and *species*. These two items tell you to look for a sentence in the passage that has both a number and the word *species*. Then you can find the sentence that provides the correct information. You don't have to re-read the entire passage—in fact, you can't, because you will run out of time for other questions. Instead, *skim* through the paragraphs looking for your key words.

In addition, you can use the **structure** of the passage to help you find the correct information. If you read carefully, you probably noticed that the paragraph talks about species first, then venom, then bites. Thus, you can use your understanding of the structure to guide you to the place to find the correct answer.

To find specific facts and details, use these two guidelines:

1. Look for *key words* in the question to tell you exactly what information to look for in the passage.
2. Think about the *structure* of the passage and where that information is likely to be located.

You can use the same approach for all three types of questions. For example, imagine you are asked: In which sentence does the author state how many snakebites result in death?

Find the key words in the question: *how many, bites,* and *death.* Then, scan the paragraph looking for the sentence that discusses the number of deadly bites.

Note that the key word might not be the exact word in the passage. For example, the question might be phrased as follows:

In which sentence does the author state the number of snakebites that are fatal?

In this case, your key words are *number, bites,* and *fatal.* But you won't find "fatal" anywhere in the passage. As you scan, then, you need to keep your eyes open for the key words *and* other words that might address the same idea. For *fatal*, for example, you might scan for the words *death, kill,* and *deadly* to find the correct answer to this question.

Again, if you noticed the structure of the paragraph as you read, you would also know to look at the end of the paragraph.

Practice 3

Read the passage below carefully and then answer the questions that follow. [Answers and explanations to all practice questions are located in Appendix A.]

(1) The Industrial Revolution was essentially a rapid change in the method of production of material goods. (2) Products once made by hand were now able to be produced by machine or

by chemical processes. (3) The Industrial Revolution transformed Western society, creating an international capitalist economy, urbanization, labor reforms, public education, and labor specialization.

(4) While the pace of change during the Industrial Revolution was indeed very rapid, the Industrial Revolution itself stretched over a rather long period of time—from the mid-1700s through World War I (1914). (5) In the first century of the Industrial Revolution, the country undergoing the most dramatic change was England. (6) After 1850, the Industrial Revolution spread rapidly throughout Europe.

(7) Several key discoveries and inventions enabled the Industrial Revolution to take place. (8) These included machines and tools like the cotton gin, the radio, the circular saw, the cylindrical press, and the steam engine. (9) Cement, dynamite, and aluminum were invented, as were the bleaching and papermaking processes.

1. The Industrial Revolution took place during which years?
   a. 1700–1850
   b. 1850–1914
   c. 1700–1914
   d. 1850–today

2. Which of the following was NOT an effect of the Industrial Revolution?
   a. advances in medical technology
   b. mechanization of hand labor
   c. development of a public education system
   d. specialization of labor

3. In which sentence does the author describe machines developed during the Industrial Revolution?
   a. sentence (2)
   b. sentence (7)
   c. sentence (8)
   d. sentence (9)

Recognizing Structure and Organizational Patterns

As already mentioned, when you are looking for specific information in a passage, it's often helpful to use the structure of the passage as a guide. Recognizing structural patterns can also help you answer the TOEFL exam sentence insertion questions. If you can identify organizational strategies and recognize transitional phrases, you will have a better chance of answering these questions correctly.

When writers write, they generally use one of several basic organizational patterns. These basic patterns help writers organize their ideas effectively. The four most common patterns are:

- chronological order
- order of importance
- comparison and contrast
- cause and effect

CHRONOLOGICAL ORDER

When writers use *time* to organize their ideas, it is called **chronological order.** They describe events in the order in which they did happen, will happen, or should happen. Much of what you read is organized in this way. Historical texts, instructions and procedures, and essays about personal experiences usually use this structure as the overall organizing principle. The practice passage about bicycles, for example, follows this pattern.

Passages organized by chronology provide us with lots of clues to help us follow the passage of time. They use **transitional words and phrases** to guide us through the text. The transitions help us see when things happened and in what order and help us follow along when the passage shifts from one period of time to another. Transitional words and phrases keep events linked together in the proper order.

Here is a list of some of the most common chronological transitions:

first, second, third, etc.	before	after	next	now
then	when	as soon as	immediately	suddenly
soon	during	while	meanwhile	later
in the meantime	at last	eventually	finally	afterward

ORDER OF IMPORTANCE

This organizational pattern arranges ideas by *rank* instead of time. That is, the first idea isn't what *happened* first; it's the idea that's most or least *important*. Writers can start with the most important idea and then work down the line to the least important. Or they can do the opposite: start with the least important idea and build up to the one that's most important.

Organizing ideas from most important to least important puts the most essential information first. Writers often do this when they are offering advice or when they want to be sure readers get the most important information right away. Newspaper articles, for example, generally use this structure. They begin with the most important information (the *who, what, when, where,* and *why* about the event) so readers don't have to read the whole article to get those facts.

When writers move from least to most important, they save their most important idea or piece of information for last. Writers often use this approach when they are presenting an argument. That's because this kind of structure is usually more convincing than a most-to-least organization. The more controversial the argument, the more important this structure. In an argument, you need to build your case piece by piece and win your readers over point by point. If your less important points make sense to the reader, then your more important points will come off stronger. And, as the saying goes, writers often "save the best for last" because that's where "the best" often has the most impact. In other words, the writer's **purpose** helps to determine the structure he or she uses.

Transitions are very important for this organizational pattern, too. Here's a list of the most common transitions writers use with the order of importance structure. Most of these work for both most-to-least important and least-to-most important patterns:

first and foremost	most importantly	more importantly	moreover
above all	first, second, third	last but not least	finally

COMPARISON AND CONTRAST

When you show how two or more things are similar, you are making a **comparison.** When you show how two or more things are different, you are **contrasting** them. This technique gives you a way to classify or judge the items you are analyzing. By placing two (or more) items side by side, for example, you can see how they measure up against each other. How are they similar or different? And why does it matter? For example, you might say that the film *Crouching Tiger, Hidden Dragon* was even better than *Star Wars*. Both featured warriors with special powers and a love story (comparison). But in *Crouching Tiger,* the fighters relied much more on their physical strength and agility than on powered weapons, which are plentiful in *Star Wars* (contrast). And *Crouching Tiger* featured female warriors as strong as (or even stronger than) the male fighters (contrast).

Whenever an author is comparing and contrasting two or more items, he or she is doing it for a reason. There's something the author wants to point out by putting these two items side by side. For example, we could compare the French Revolution and the American Revolution to show how they both overthrew monarchies to create a free republic.

One of the keys to a good comparison and contrast is strong transitions. It's important to let readers know when you are comparing and when you are contrasting. As a reader, it's important to watch for these transitions.

Here are some words and phrases that show similarity:

similarly	in the same way	likewise
like	in a like manner	just as
and	also	both

The following words and phrases, on the other hand, show difference:

but	on the other hand	yet
however	on the contrary	in contrast
conversely	while	unlike

CAUSE AND EFFECT

Another common organizational pattern is cause and effect. A **cause** is a person or thing that makes something happen (creates an effect). An **effect** is an event or change created by an action (or cause). A passage about cause explains *why* something took place. You might ask, for example, "What caused the Industrial Revolution?" A passage about effect, on the other hand, explains *what happened after* something took place. What happened as a result of the Industrial Revolution? How did it affect the economy? Daily life? Education?

Just as certain key words indicate whether you're comparing or contrasting, other key words indicate whether things are causes or effects. Here is a partial list of words and phrases that indicate cause and effect:

WORDS INDICATING CAUSE:

because (of)   created (by)

since   caused (by)

WORDS INDICATING EFFECT:

therefore   so

hence   consequently

as a result

HOW THIS CAN HELP YOU ON THE TOEFL EXAM

Familiarity with organizational patterns can help you in several ways as you prepare for and take the TOEFL exam. Once you recognize an organizational pattern, you can anticipate what's ahead. This often makes it easier to understand and remember what you read. It also makes it easier to find specific information in the text for those specific fact/detail questions.

When you know the structure of a passage, you can also make better decisions about where to insert new information. For example, read this passage:

The current measure used to calculate poverty levels was introduced in 1963. At that time, the poverty line for a family of two adults and two children was about $3,100. In 1992, there were 36.9 million people, or 14.5 percent of the U.S. population, with incomes below the poverty line. (1) A proposed new way of measuring poverty levels would take into account the effects of work-related expenses such as transportation and child-care costs.

(2) By including these costs, fewer people in families receiving cash welfare would fall under the poverty line while a greater percentage of people in working families would be categorized as poor. Specifically, people in families receiving cash welfare would make up 30 percent of the poor under the new measure, compared with 40 percent under the current measure. (3) In contrast, people in working families would make up 59 percent of the poor under the new measure, compared with 51 percent under the current measure. (4)

Here is an example of a question you may encounter on the TOEFL exam.

The following sentence can be added to this passage:

The new measure would have two important effects.

Where would this sentence best fit in the passage? Choose the number to indicate where you would add the sentence to the passage.
a. (1)
b. (2)
c. (3)
d. (4)

Because the sentence to insert clearly sets up a cause/effect structure, it gives you a strong clue about where it best belongs. The sentence will make the most sense if it comes right before the passage discusses the effects of the new measure. Therefore, the best answer is choice **b**—at the beginning of the second paragraph.

Practice 4

Read the following passage carefully. [Answers and explanations to all practice questions are located in Appendix A.]

The coast of the State of Maine is one of the most irregular in the world. A straight line running from the southernmost city in Maine, Kittery, to the northernmost coastal city, Eastport, would measure about 225 miles. If you followed the coastline between the same two cities, you would travel more than ten times as far. (1) This irregularity is the result of what is called a *drowned coastline*. (2) The term comes from the glacial activity of the ice age. (3) As the glacier descended, it expended enormous force on those mountains and they sank into the sea. (4)

The following sentence can be added to this passage:

At that time, the whole area that is now Maine was part of a mountain range that towered above the sea.

Where would this sentence best fit in the passage? Choose the number to indicate where you would add the sentence to the passage.

a. (1)

b. (2)

c. (3)

d. (4)

Making Inferences

Inferences are conclusions that we draw based upon evidence. For example, if you look up at the sky and see heavy black rain clouds, you might logically infer that it is going to rain. Reading comprehension tests like the TOEFL exam will often ask you to draw conclusions based upon what you read in the passage.

The key to drawing the right conclusions (making the right inferences) is the same as the key to finding the meaning of unfamiliar vocabulary words. You have to look for clues in the context. The best clues typically come from the writer's **word choice**.

WORD CHOICE

Often the best clues to meaning come from the specific words a writer chooses to describe people, places, and things. The writer's word choice (also called *diction*) can reveal an awful lot about how he or she feels about the subject.

By looking closely at word choice, you will find clues that can help you better understand the text. Word choice clues can come in the following forms:

- particular words and phrases that the author uses
- the way those words and phrases are arranged in sentences
- word or sentence patterns that are repeated
- important details about people, places, and things

To see how word choice reveals the writer's attitude, read the two sentences below:

A: A school uniform policy would reduce disciplinary problems.

B: A school uniform policy would minimize disciplinary problems.

It's not hard to see the difference between these sentences. In sentence A, the writer says the policy will *reduce* disciplinary problems; sentence B, on the other hand, uses the word *minimize*. No big deal, right? After all, both sentences say that the uniform policy will result in fewer disciplinary problems. But there is a difference. One sentence is much stronger than the other because one word is actually much stronger than the other. *To minimize* is to reduce to the smallest possible amount. Thus, while both writers agree that a uniform dress code would lessen disciplinary problems, the writer of sentence B feels that it would nearly eliminate them. The writer doesn't need to spell this out for you because his *word choice* should make his position clear.

DENOTATION AND CONNOTATION

Even words that seem to mean the same thing have subtly different meanings and sometimes not-so-subtle effects. For example, look at the words *slim* and *thin.* If you say your aunt is *thin,* that means one thing. If you say she is *slim,* that means something a little bit different. That's because *slim* has a different **connotation** than *thin.*

Connotation is a word's *suggested* or implied meaning; it's what the word makes you think or feel. *Slim* and *thin* have almost the same **denotation**—their dictionary definition—but *slim* suggests more grace and class than *thin.* Slim is a very positive word. It suggests that your aunt is healthy and fit. *Thin,* however, does not. *Thin* suggests that your aunt may be a little bit too skinny for her health. *Thin* and *slim,* then, have different connotations. So the word you choose to describe your aunt can tell others a lot.

Practice 5

[Answers and explanations to all practice questions are located in Appendix A.]

Part 1. To help you become more aware of connotation, rank the following sets of words. Give the word with the strongest connotation a score of (1) and the word with the weakest (most neutral) connotation a (4).

1. He is feeling a little _____ today.

_____ down

_____ depressed

_____ discouraged

_____ low

2. She told him a _____.

_____ lie

_____ fib

_____ half-truth

_____ untruth

3. The situation was _____.

_____ risky

_____ perilous

_____ life-threatening

_____ dangerous

Part 2. Read the paired sentences below. Use your observations about word choice to answer the questions that follow.

Pair 1

A: The French Revolution of 1789 was inspired by the American Revolution of 1776.

B: The French Revolution of 1789 was modeled after the American Revolution of 1776.
   1. Which sentence suggests that the French and American Revolutions had similar causes?
   2. Which sentence suggests that the French and American Revolutions were similar in method?

Pair 2

A: Nearly two million Americans suffer from bipolar disorder.

B: Nearly two million Americans have bipolar disorder.
   1. Which sentence presents bipolar disorder as a more serious condition?
   2. Which sentence appears to be more objective?

▶ Putting It All Together: Reading Comprehension Practice Passages

Now it's time to practice all of the reading comprehension skills you have reviewed in this chapter. There are two practice passages below. Read each one carefully and then answer the questions that follow. The questions are just like those you will see on the TOEFL exam. You will find the Answer Key in Appendix A.

Comprehensive Practice Passage 1

There are three different kinds of burns: first degree, second degree, and third degree. Each type of burn requires a different type of medical treatment.

The least serious burn is the first degree burn. This burn causes the skin to turn red but does not cause blistering. A mild sunburn is a good example of a first degree burn, and, like a mild sunburn, first degree burns generally do not require medical treatment other than a gentle cooling of the burned skin with ice or cold tap water.

Second degree burns, on the other hand, do cause blistering of the skin and should be treated immediately. These burns should be immersed in warm water and then wrapped in a sterile dressing or bandage. (Do not apply butter or grease to these burns. Despite the old wives' tale, butter does not help burns heal but actually increases the chances of infection.) If a second degree burn covers a large part of the body, then the victim should be taken to the hospital immediately for medical care.

Third degree burns are those that char the skin and turn it black or burn so deeply that the skin shows white. These burns usually result from direct contact with flames and have a great chance of becoming infected. All third degree burn victims should receive immediate hospital care. Burns should not be immersed in water, and charred clothing should not be removed from the victim as it may also remove the skin. If possible, a sterile dressing or bandage should be applied to burns before the victim is transported to the hospital.

1. The main idea of this passage is best expressed in which sentence?
   a. Third degree burns are very serious.
   b. There are three different kinds of burns.
   c. Some burns require medical treatment.
   d. Each type of burn requires a different type of treatment.

2. A mild sunburn should be treated by:
   a. removing charred clothing
   b. immersing it in warm water and wrapping it in a sterile bandage
   c. getting immediate medical attention
   d. gently cooling the burned skin with cool water

3. Which of the following is NOT a recommended treatment for third degree burns?
   a. Immerse in warm water.
   b. Get immediate hospital care.
   c. Apply a sterile bandage.
   d. Keep charred clothing on the victim.

4. The word *it* in the first sentence of paragraph 4 refers to:
   a. a third-degree burn
   b. the skin
   c. charred clothing
   d. infection

5. The phrase *old wives' tale* in paragraph 3 could best be replaced by which word or phrase?
   a. good advice
   b. lie
   c. ancient story
   d. popular belief

6. Where in the passage does the author describe the characteristics of second-degree burns?

   a. at the end of paragraph 2
   b. at the beginning of paragraph 3
   c. at the end of paragraph 3
   d. at the beginning of paragraph 4

Comprehensive Practice Passage 2

(The numbers in the text are for the sentence insertion question.)

There are two types of diabetes: insulin-dependent (Type I) and non-insulin-dependent (Type II). An estimated 14 million people in the United States have diabetes, and most (90–95%) have the non-insulin-dependent type. Unlike the symptoms of Type I diabetes, the symptoms of Type II often develop gradually and are hard to identify at first. (1) Therefore, nearly half of all people with Type II diabetes do not know they have it. (2) While the causes, onset of symptoms, short-term effects, and treatments of the two types differ, both types of diabetes can cause the same long-term health problems. (3)

The most important problem is the way both types affect the body's ability to use digested food for energy. Diabetes does not interfere with digestion, but it does prevent the body from using an important product of digestion—*glucose* (commonly known as sugar)—for energy. After a meal, the normal digestive system breaks some food down into glucose. The blood carries glucose throughout the body, causing blood glucose levels to rise. In response to this rise, the hormone *insulin* is released into the blood stream. Insulin signals the body tissues to metabolize, or burn, the glucose for fuel, which causes blood glucose levels to return to normal. The glucose that the body does not use right away is stored in the liver, muscle tissue, or fat.

In both types of diabetes, however, this normal process malfunctions. A gland called the *pancreas,* found just behind the stomach, makes insulin. In people with insulin-dependent diabetes, the pancreas does not produce insulin at all. These patients must have daily insulin injections to survive. People with non-insulin dependent diabetes usually produce some insulin in their pancreas, but the body's tissues do not respond very well to the insulin signal and therefore do not metabolize the glucose properly. This condition is also known as *insulin resistance.*

There's no cure for diabetes yet. (4) However, there are ways to <u>alleviate</u> its symptoms. In 1986, a National Institutes of Health panel of experts recommended that the best treatment for Type II diabetes is a diet that helps one maintain a normal weight and balances all food groups. Many experts, including those in the American Diabetes Association, recommend that 50–60 percent of daily calories come from carbohydrates, 12–20 percent from protein, and no more than 30% from fat. Foods that are rich in carbohydrates, like breads, cereals, fruits, and vegetables, break down into glucose during digestion, causing blood glucose to rise. Additionally, studies have shown that cooked foods raise blood glucose higher than raw foods.

7. What is the author's main purpose in this passage?

    a. to show readers how to prevent diabetes

    b. to show the differences between Type I and II diabetes

    c. to describe the best diet for people with diabetes

    d. to describe the health problem caused by both types of diabetes

8. The word *alleviate* in paragraph 4 is closest in meaning to

    a. get rid of.

    b. reduce.

    c. increase.

    d. medicate.

9. Insulin is produced by

    a. the stomach.

    b. the pancreas.

    c. the blood.

    d. the liver.

10. Which of the following is NOT true of glucose?

    a. It is produced from food during digestion.

    b. It is carried in the bloodstream.

    c. It is burned by the body for energy.

    d. It is a hormone produced by the body.

11. The passage suggests that:

    a. A diet too heavy in carbohydrates is bad for people with diabetes.

    b. People with diabetes need extra carbohydrates in their diet.

    c. Diabetes is not really a very serious disease.

    d. People with diabetes should lose weight.

12. What does the author mean by the statement **Diabetes does not interfere with digestion, but it does prevent the body from using an important product of digestion—*glucose* (commonly known as sugar)—for energy?**

    a. Diabetes prevents the body from digesting food.

    b. Diabetes is triggered by too much sugar in the body.

    c. Diabetes causes the body to burn too much glucose for energy.

    d. Diabetes blocks the body's ability to process sugar during digestion.

13. The following sentence can be inserted into the passage:

But it is very important for people to be aware that they have this disease.

Where would this sentence best fit in the passage? Choose the number to indicate where you would add the sentence to the passage.

a. (1)

b. (2)

c. (3)

d. (4)

3 ▶ Structure: Grammar and Style

As you can imagine, you will do a great deal of writing in college. To do well in an American school, you will need to write in clear, grammatically correct English. In this chapter, you will learn exactly what the structure section of the TOEFL exam is like. You will also review and practice basic grammatical rules and patterns so you can write correctly and perform well on the exam.

WHEN WE ARE communicating with others, speaking has several advantages over writing. For one thing, speaking enables dialogue. If we don't understand what the speaker is saying, we can ask the speaker to repeat, rephrase, or clarify his or her ideas. For another, when we speak, we have much more freedom to play with grammar and stylistic conventions. We can use slang, clip off endings of words, and state incomplete or run-on thoughts. Because we are speaking, often formulating our thoughts as we go, it is natural and even acceptable to make occasional grammatical mistakes. And when we do, we have the chance to correct ourselves before we continue.

Not so with writing. Writing necessarily distances us from our audience, and we cannot correct ourselves as we go along or backtrack if our reader doesn't understand what we have written. When we write, therefore, we need to be clear and correct from the start. Otherwise, our readers may not be able to understand our message.

Because you will do an enormous amount of writing in college—including lab reports, research papers, and essays—admissions officers need to know that you can communicate clearly and correctly in written English. That's why Section II of the TOEFL exam tests your knowledge of English grammar and style.

► The TOEFL Exam Structure Section: What to Expect

Section II: Structure does not require you to actually *write* grammatically and stylistically correct sentences. You will have that opportunity in Section IV: Writing (or the Test of Written English™ [TWE®] if you take the paper-based exam). Instead, Section II presents you with a series of sentences in which you have to correctly fill in the blank or identify a grammatical mistake.

These sentences will cover a wide range of topics, including history, biology, culture, and art. But you do not need background knowledge in the subject to answer the questions correctly. The sentences will provide enough context to make their meaning clear, but the actual subject of the sentence is not important. What matters is that you can recognize and correct errors in English grammar and style.

► Kinds of Structure Questions on the TOEFL Exam

On both the computer-based and paper TOEFL exams, you will find two types of questions:

Type 1: Incomplete sentences. These sentences will have a blank and ask you to select the *correct* word or phrase to put in that blank. On the paper-based TOEFL exam, these questions are called Structure questions.

   Examples:

1. It is illegal _____ cars on a two-lane road when there is a solid yellow dividing line.
   a. passes
   b. passing
   c. to pass
   d. when passing

2. After a female seahorse produces eggs, she gives them to her mate, _____ fertilizes them and carries them in his pouch until they are ready to be born.
   a. he
   b. who
   c. which
   d. while

   Answers: 1-c, 2-b.

Type 2: Sentences with underlined words or phrases. These sentences will have several underlined words or phrases. You will be asked to choose which of the underlined words or phrases is *incorrect*. On the paper-based TOEFL exam, these questions are called Written Expression questions.

Computer-Based Test vs. Paper-Based Test

THERE are a few important differences between the structure sections of the new computer-based TOEFL exam and the old paper-based exam. The kinds of questions are the same, but the computer-based test offers fewer questions. More important, the questions on the computer exam will be selected according to your level of proficiency. Your first question will be "average" in difficulty. The next question will be easier or harder, depending upon how you answered the first question. The rest of the questions will follow this pattern. Throughout the structure section on the computer-based test, the level of difficulty of each question will be based upon your answer to the previous question.

This chart compares the structure sections of the two tests:

Computer-Based TOEFL Exam ("Structure")	Supplemental Paper-Based TOEFL Exam ("Structure and Written Expression")
15–20 minutes	25 minutes
20–25 questions	40 questions
Question types (see "Kinds of Structure Questions" below) are not divided into sections. Incomplete sentence and sentences with underlined words and phrases will be presented at random.	Question types are divided into two sections: Part A consists of 15 incomplete sentences ("structure" questions) and Part B consists of 25 sentences with underlined words and phrases ("written expression" questions).
The computer selects questions based on your level of proficiency.	All test-takers answer the same questions.
Once you submit an answer, you cannot go back to previous questions.	You can return to previous questions and change your answer.
Your score on this section is combined with your score on the essay in the writing section.	Your score on this section is not combined with your score on the essay in the writing section (Test of Written English™).

Source: *Barron's Passkey to the TOEFL®*, 4th ed., 2001.

Examples:

3. Frederick Law Olmsted, who <u>designed</u> Manhattan's Central Park, <u>wanting</u> the park <u>to be</u> a "democratic
                                A   B   C

playground" <u>where</u> everyone was equal.
              D

  a. A
  b. B
  c. C
  d. D

4. A <u>lack in</u> folic acid, <u>especially in</u> early pregnancy, <u>can</u> lead to serious <u>birth</u> defects.
      A   B   C   D

    a. A
    b. B
    c. C
    d. D

    Answers: 3-b, 4-a.

▶ Grammar and Style Review

Now that you have a better idea of what to expect on the structure section of the TOEFL exam, it's time to review some basic English grammar patterns and rules. This review and the practice exercises throughout the chapter will help you write more clearly and correctly and better prepare for the exam.

The Basic Unit of Writing: Sentences and Sentence Structure

When we write, we express our ideas in sentences. But what *is* a sentence, anyway?

SUBJECTS, PREDICATES, AND OBJECTS

A sentence is the basic unit of thought in the English language. It is composed of two essential parts—a **subject** and a **predicate**—and it must express a complete thought. The subject of a sentence tells us who or what the sentence is about. The predicate tells us something *about* the subject. Thus, in the following sentence:

    The snow is falling.

The word *snow* is the subject. It tells us what the sentence is about—who or what performed the action of the sentence. The verb phrase *is falling* is the predicate. It tells us the action performed by (or information about) the subject.

The subject of a sentence can be **singular** or **compound** (plural):

I ate a large pizza.	*Ted* and *I* ate a large pizza.
singular subject	compound subject (two subjects performing the action)

The predicate can also be singular or compound:

I ate a large pizza.	*I ate a large pizza* and *drank a liter of soda.*
singular predicate	compound predicate (two actions performed by the subject)

In many sentences, someone or something "receives" the action expressed in the predicate. This person or thing is called the **direct object**. In the sentences below, the subject and predicate are separated by a slash (/) and the direct object is underlined:

I / ate <u>a large pizza.</u>	(The pizza receives the action of being eaten.)
Jack / loves <u>Jill</u>.	(Jill receives the action of being loved.)

Sentences can also have an **indirect object**: a person or thing who "receives" the direct object. In the sentences below, the direct object is underlined and the indirect object is in bold:

*I / gave **Xiomara** <u>a gift.</u>*	(Xiomara receives the gift; the gift receives the action of being given.)
*The teacher / threw the **children** <u>a surprise party.</u>*	(The children receive the party; the party receives the action of being thrown.)

Practice 1

For each of the following sentences, please:

A. Put a slash ("/") between the subject and the predicate.
B. Identify whether the subject is singular or compound.
C. Identify whether the predicate is singular or compound.
D. Underline any direct objects.
E. Circle any indirect objects.

You will find the Answer Key in Appendix A.

1. Tobias washed his car.

2. My boss gave me a huge raise.

3. The engineer measured the water level in the reservoir and tested it for contaminants.

4. Horace and Renee both told the detective a different story.

INDEPENDENT AND DEPENDENT CLAUSES

A **clause** is a group of words that has a subject and a predicate (clauses can have direct and indirect objects, too). A clause that expresses a complete thought is called an **independent clause;** it can stand on its own as a sentence. A **dependent clause,** on the other hand, cannot stand alone because it expresses an incomplete thought. When a dependent clause stands alone, the result is a **sentence fragment.**

Independent clause: *It rained.*
Dependent clause: *Because it rained.*

Notice how the dependent clause is incomplete; it requires an additional thought to make a complete sentence. The independent thought, however, can stand alone.

What makes the dependent clause above *dependent* is the word *because. Because* is one of many **subordinating conjunctions** like the following:

SUBORDINATING CONJUNCTIONS:

after	before	that	when
although	if	though	where
as, as if	once	unless	wherever
because	since	until	while

When a clause has a subordinating conjunction, it must be connected to an independent clause to become a complete thought:

Because it rained,   *the game was cancelled.*
dependent clause   independent clause
I was so hungry   *that I ate a whole pizza.*
independent clause   dependent clause

A sentence with both a dependent and independent clause is called a **complex sentence.** Both of the sentences above are complex sentences.

When two *independent* clauses are combined, the result is a **compound sentence** like the following:

It rained, so the game was cancelled.

The most common way to join two independent clauses is with a comma and a **coordinating conjunction:** *and, but, or, nor, for, so, yet.* Independent clauses can also be joined with a semi-colon if the ideas in the sentences are closely related.

I was starving, <u>so</u> I ate a whole pizza.

The dog needs to be fed daily<u>, but</u> the fish only needs to be fed every other day.

He is from Australia<u>;</u> she is from New Zealand.

PHRASES AND MODIFIERS

Sentences are often "filled out" by **phrases** and **modifiers.** Phrases are groups of words that *do not* have both a subject and predicate. Modifiers are words and phrases that qualify or describe people, places, things and actions. The most common phrases are **prepositional phrases,** which consist of a preposition and a noun or pronoun (e.g., *in the kitchen*). Modifiers include **adjectives** (e.g., *dark, stormy*) and **adverbs** (e.g., *slowly, carefully*). In the examples below, the prepositional phrases are underlined and the modifiers are in bold:

*I gave Xiomara a **beautiful, hand-made** gift <u>for her **sixteenth**</u> birthday.*

***Yesterday** I ate a **large** pizza <u>with mushrooms and anchovies.</u>*

*<u>On Friday,</u> it rained **all day,** so the **baseball** game was cancelled <u>by the league.</u>*

Prepositions: A Short List

PREPOSITIONS are extremely important. They help us understand how objects relate to each other in space and time. But they can also be one of the most difficult aspects of a foreign language to learn. Here are the more common prepositions. See page 83 for notes about the most common prepositional idioms.

about	beside	inside	through
above	besides	into	throughout
across	between	like	till
after	beyond	near	to
against	by	of	toward
around	down	off	under
at	during	on	until
before	except	out	up
behind	for	outside	upon
below	from	over	with
beneath	in	since	without

Practice 2

For the following sentences, please:

A. Place brackets "[ ]" around any dependent clauses.
B. Underline any prepositional phrases.
C. Circle any modifiers.

1. Since interest rates have dropped considerably in the last month, it would be wise to refinance the mortgage on your new home.

2. I finally reached Tom in his office, and he said he would ship the redesigned brochures by express mail.

3. When I mailed the 200-page manuscript to my editor, I didn't realize that the pages were completely out of order.

4. Whether you are ready or not, the chemistry test is tomorrow at 9:00 in Room 213.

5. The seven-foot-tall ostrich is the fastest two-legged animal on Earth.

Parts of Speech

A word's part of speech determines its **function** and **form.** The word *quiet,* for example, can be either a verb or an adjective; it changes to *quietly* when it is an adverb. Be sure you know the different parts of speech and the job each part of speech performs in a sentence. The following table offers a quick reference guide for the main parts of speech.

PART OF SPEECH	FUNCTION	EXAMPLES
noun	names a person, place, thing, or concept	*girl, Eleanor, street, Walsh Avenue, calculator, happiness*
pronoun	takes the place of a noun so that noun does not have to be repeated	*I, you, he, she, us, they, this, that, themselves, somebody, who, which*
verb	describes an action, occurrence, or state of being	*jump, becomes, is, seemed, clamoring*
helping verb (also called auxiliary verb)	combines with other verbs (main verbs) to create verb phrases that help indicate tenses	forms of *be, do* and *have*; *can, could, may, might, must, shall, should, will, would*
adjective	describes nouns and pronouns; can also identify or quantify	*red, small, glorious, unexpected; that* (e.g., *that car*); *several* (e.g., *several dogs*)
adverb	describes verbs, adjectives, other adverbs, or entire clauses	*slowly, happily, always, very, yesterday*
preposition	expresses the relationship in time or space between words in a sentence	*in, on, around, above, between, underneath, beside, with, upon* (see list on page 83).

The hunter approached the white-tailed deer silently,
   noun   verb   adjective   noun   adverb

but the deer had sensed   him and escaped   into   the woods.
            helping verb pronoun   verb preposition   noun

Verbs

Verbs are the agents of action in a sentence. They are the "heart" of a sentence because they express the **action** or **state of being** of the subject:

> It **rains** a lot in Seattle. (action)
> I **feel** really good about this deal. (state of being)
> The poor cat **is** starving. (state of being)
> Chester **smiled** broadly. (action)

Verbs have five basic forms:

1. **Infinitive base:** the base form of the verb plus the word *to*.

    to go   *to be*   *to desire*   *to arrange*

    To indicate tenses of regular verbs (when the action of the verb did occur, is occurring, or will occur), we use the base form of the verb and add the appropriate tense endings.

2. **Present tense:** the verb form that expresses what is happening now.

    *I **am** glad you **are** here.*
    *Chester **smiles** a lot.*

    The present tense of regular verbs is formed as follows:

	SINGULAR	PLURAL
first person (I/we)	base form (*dream*)	base form (*dream*)
second person (you)	base form (*dream*)	base form (*dream*)
third person (he/she/it, they)	base form + *-s/-es* (*dreams*)	base form (*dream*)

3. **Present participle:** the verb form that describes what is happening now. It ends in *-ing* and is accompanied by a helping verb such as *is*.

    Chester <u>is smiling</u> again.
    They <u>are watching</u> the stock market very carefully.

    NOTE: Words that end in *-ing* don't always function as verbs. Sometimes they act as nouns and are called **gerunds.** They can also function as adjectives (called **participial phrases**).

Present participle (verb):	*He <u>is eating</u> the plastic fruit!*
Gerund (noun):	*That plastic fruit is not for <u>eating</u>!*
Participial phrase (adjective):	*The <u>sleeping</u> baby awoke when the phone rang.*

    (You will learn more about gerunds later in this chapter.)

4. **Past tense:** the verb form that expresses what happened in the past.

> It _rained_ four inches yesterday.
> The cat _felt_ better after it _ate._

5. **Past participle:** the verb form that describes an action that happened in the past and is used with a helping verb, such as _has, have,_ or _had._

> It _had_ _rained_ for days.
> Chester _has_ not _smiled_ for days.

REGULAR VERBS

Regular verbs follow a standard set of rules for forming the present participle, past tense, and past participle forms. The present participle is formed by adding _-ing._ The past and past participle are formed by adding _-ed._ If the verb ends with the letter _e,_ just add _d._ If the verb ends with the letter _y,_ for the past tense, change the _y_ to an _i_ and add _-ed._ Here are some examples:

PRESENT	PRESENT PARTICIPLE	PAST	PAST PARTICIPLE
connect	connecting	connected	connected
exercise	exercising	exercised	exercised
follow	following	followed	followed
multiply	multiplying	multiplied	multiplied
notice	noticing	noticed	noticed
solve	solving	solved	solved
wash	washing	washed	washed

Some verbs in the English language have the same present, past, and past participle form. Here is a partial list of those verbs followed by several examples:

SAME PRESENT, PAST, AND PAST PARTICIPLE FORM:

bet	hit	set
bid	hurt	shut
burst	put	spread
cost	quit	upset
cut	read	

Present:	_I **bet** that he will be late._
Past:	_Yesterday I **bet** $20 that he would be late._
Past participle:	_Yesterday I had **bet** $20 that he would be late._
Present:	_That antique lamp **cost** Jude over $500._
Past:	_That antique lamp **cost** Jude over $500._
Past participle:	_That antique lamp had **cost** Jude over $500._

IRREGULAR VERBS

About 150 verbs in the English language are *irregular*. They don't follow the standard rules for changing tense. We can divide these verbs into three categories:

- irregular verbs with the same *past* and *past participle* forms
- irregular verbs with three distinct forms
- irregular verbs with the same *present* and *past participle* forms.

The table below lists the most common irregular verbs.

Present	Past	Past Participle	Present	Past	Past Participle
Same past and past participle forms:			buy	bought	bought
bite	bit	bit	catch	caught	caught
dig	dug	dug	fight	fought	fought
bleed	bled	bled	teach	taught	taught
hear	heard	heard	think	thought	thought
hold	held	held	feed	fed	fed
light	lit	lit	flee	fled	fled
meet	met	met	find	found	found
pay	paid	paid	grind	ground	ground
say	said	said	**Three distinct forms:**		
sell	sold	sold	begin	began	begun
tell	told	told	ring	rang	rung
shine	shone	shone	sing	sang	sung
shoot	shot	shot	spring	sprang	sprung
sit	sat	sat	do	did	done
spin	spun	spun	go	went	gone
spit	spat	spat	am	was	been
swear	swore	swore	is	was	been
tear	tore	tore	see	saw	seen
creep	crept	crept	drink	drank	drunk
deal	dealt	dealt	shrink	shrank	shrunk
keep	kept	kept	sink	sank	sunk
kneel	knelt	knelt	stink	stank	stunk
leave	left	left	swear	swore	sworn
mean	meant	meant	tear	tore	torn
send	sent	sent	wear	wore	worn
sleep	slept	slept	blow	blew	blown
spend	spent	spent	draw	drew	drawn
bring	brought	brought	fly	flew	flown

Present	Past	Past Participle	Present	Past	Past Participle
grow	grew	grown	get	got	gotten
know	knew	known	give	gave	given
throw	threw	thrown	forgive	forgave	forgiven
drive	drove	driven	forsake	forsook	forsaken
strive	strove	striven	hide	hid	hidden
choose	chose	chosen	ride	rode	ridden
rise	rose	risen	write	wrote	written
break	broke	broken	freeze	froze	frozen
speak	spoke	spoken	steal	stole	stolen
fall	fell	fallen	*Same present and past participle forms:*		
shake	shook	shaken	come	came	come
take	took	taken	overcome	overcame	overcome
forget	forgot	forgotten	run	ran	run

SPECIAL CASE: TO BE

The verb *to be* can pose special problems because the principal parts are formed in such unusual ways. The table below shows how to conjugate *to be*:

SUBJECT	PRESENT	PAST	PAST PARTICIPLE
I	am	was	have been
you	are	were	have been
he, she, it	is	was	has been
we	are	were	have been
they	are	were	have been

HELPING VERBS

Helping verbs (also called **auxiliary verbs**) are very important. They help signal exactly when an action took place or will take place. They also suggest very specific meanings, such as the subject's ability or intention to do something. The following table lists the helping verbs, their forms, and their meanings.

PRESENT & FUTURE	PAST	MEANING	EXAMPLES
will, shall	would	intention	*I will go to the store right away.* *She said she would give you the report.*
can	could	ability	*They can do the job right.* *Fatima could read by the time she was three.*
may, might, can, could	could, might	permission	*You may be excused.* *We could leave early if we want to.*
should	should + have + past participle	recommendation	*The nurse said I should lie down and rest.* *We should have given her better directions.*
must, have (to)	had (to)	necessity	*Doctors must write very detailed notes regarding each patient visit.* *They had to get to the bank before it closed.*
should	should + have + past participle	expectation	*The doctor should have sent you a copy of his report.* *They should have finished at the bank by now.*
may, might	might + have + past participle	possibility	*The rebels may agree to a cease-fire.* *The revolution might not have succeeded without their support.*

Practice 3

Answer the questions below. If the question has a blank, choose the *correct* answer to fill in the blank. If the question has four underlined words or phrases, choose the underlined word or phrase that is *incorrect*. You will find the Answer Key in Appendix A.

1. Kay and Sandy are _____ the retirement dinner this year.
  a. to organize
  b. organize
  c. organizing
  d. organized

2. Lyle _____ down as he approached the intersection.
  a. to slow
  b. slow
  c. slowing
  d. slowed

3. Last month, Lillian _____ her bills with her credit card.
   a. to pay
   b. pay
   c. paying
   d. paid

4. Jack _____ working overtime for the last three weeks.
   a. is
   b. was
   c. has been
   d. did

5. The band on my watch _____.
   a. break
   b. broke
   c. did breaking
   d. broken

6. He believes we _____ go to a specialist right away.
   a. will
   b. must
   c. should
   d. would

7. Be very careful; that dog _____ bite.
   a. may
   b. should
   c. would
   d. can

8. The thieves _____ before the police could catch them.
   a. flew
   b. fled
   c. flied
   d. fleed

9. Neither the president nor the senators _____ the outcome of the vote.
   a. to know
   b. know
   c. are knowing
   d. have known

10. Because the rain <u>fell</u> all night, the <u>clogged</u> drain pipe <u>bursted</u> and <u>flooded</u> the house.
                        A   B   C   D
   a. A
   b. B
   c. C
   d. D

SUBJUNCTIVE MOOD

The **subjunctive mood** of verbs is used to express something that is wished for or that is contrary to fact. The subjunctive form of *was* is *were*. We often forget to use the subjunctive when we speak, but it is the grammatically correct form we should use in this situation. And it's quite possible that you will see a question about the subjunctive on the TOEFL exam.

> *If you <u>were</u> a pet fish, you would be entirely dependent upon human beings.* (You are not a pet fish.)
> *If Andre <u>were</u> more responsible, he could be trusted with this job.* (Andre is not responsible.)

TROUBLESOME VERBS

Three sets of verbs are particularly troublesome, even for native speakers of English: *lie/lay, sit/set,* and *rise/raise.* The key to knowing which one to use is remembering which verb in each pair needs an object. For example, *lie* is an action that the subject of the sentence "performs" on itself: *I will lie down.* The verb *lay,* on the other hand, is an action that the subject of the sentence performs on an object: *He will lay the baby down in the crib.*

    lie: to rest or recline (subject only)
    lay: to put or place (needs an object)
                  Go lie down if you're tired.
                  Lay the books down on the table.
    sit: to rest (subject only)
    set: to put or place (needs an object)
                  I'd like to sit at the corner table, please.
                  He set the books on the table in the corner.
    rise: to go up (subject only)
    raise: to move something up (needs an object)
                  This far north, the sun rises at 4:30.
                  The minimum amount to open an account has been raised from $50 to $100.

The basic forms of these verbs can also be a bit tricky. The following table shows how each verb is conjugated.

PRESENT	PRESENT PARTICIPLE (with *am, is, are*)	PAST	PAST PARTICIPLE (with *have, has, had*)
lie, lies	lying	lay	lain
lay, lays	laying	laid	laid
sit, sits	sitting	sat	sat
set, sets	setting	set	set
rise, rises	rising	rose	risen
raise, raises	raising	raised	raised

Consistent Tense

To help make sure your readers are clear about *when* actions occur, it's important to make sure your verbs are consistent in tense. A passage that begins in the present tense, for example, should stay in the present tense. Do not mix tenses as you write. Otherwise, your readers will be confused about whether actions are taking place in the present or took place in the past.

Incorrect: *The officer <u>unlocked</u> the trunk and <u>searches</u> for contraband.*

Correct: *The officer <u>unlocked</u> the trunk and <u>searched</u> for contraband.*

Incorrect: *When we <u>increase</u> advertising expenses, we <u>reduced</u> profits.*

Correct: *When we <u>increase</u> advertising expenses, we <u>reduce</u> profits.*

Agreement

An important element of English grammar is agreement. In all sentences, verbs should *agree* with their subjects. Singular subjects need singular verbs; plural subjects need plural verbs.

Incorrect: *He always do a very good job.* (singular subject, plural verb)

Correct: *He always does a very good job.* (singular subject, singular verb)

Incorrect: *Sally and Vladimir is going to the movies.* (plural subject, singular verb)

Correct: *Sally and Vladimir are going to the movies.* (plural subject, plural verb)

To make sure subjects and verbs agree, you need to make sure you are clear about the subject of the sentence.

One of the chairs is broken.

In this sentence, the subject is *one*, not *chairs*. *Chairs* is part of the prepositional phrase (*of the chairs*), and **subjects are never found in prepositional phrases.** Thus, the verb must be singular (*is*, not *are*) to agree with *one*.

Here are some other subject-verb agreement guidelines:

- If a compound, singular subject is connected by *and*, the verb must be plural.
- If a compound, singular subject is connected by *or* or *nor*, the verb must be singular.
- If one plural and one singular subject are connected by *or* or *nor*, the verb agrees with the closest subject.

  Both <u>Art and Elaine</u> <u>want</u> to learn more about the Industrial Revolution.

  Neither Art <u>nor</u> Elaine <u>knows</u> much about the Industrial Revolution.

  Neither Art <u>nor</u> his <u>cousins know</u> much about the Industrial Revolution.

  Neither the boys nor their coach knows much about the Industrial Revolution.

- When the subject *comes after* the verb (an **inverted sentence**), it can be tricky to determine correct subject-verb agreement. In sentences that begin with *there is* and *there are*, for example, the subject comes after the verb. The verb (is/are) must agree with that subject. Subjects come after the verb in questions, too. Make sure you correctly identify the subject of the sentence.

Incorrect:	*There's many reasons not to go.*
Correct:	*There are many reasons not to go.*

Incorrect:	*Here's the statistics they compiled.*
Correct:	*Here are the statistics they compiled.*

Incorrect:	*What is the terms of the agreement?*
Correct:	*What are the terms of the agreement?*

Gerunds and Infinitives

Two tricky aspects of English grammar are **gerunds** and **infinitives**. Gerunds, as we noted earlier, *look* like verbs because they end in *-ing,* but they actually function as nouns in sentences:

Trevor enjoys <u>traveling</u>.

Here, the "action" Trevor performs is *enjoys*. The *thing* (noun) he enjoys is *traveling*. In the following sentence, however, *traveling* is the action Trevor performs, so it is functioning as a verb:

Trevor is <u>traveling</u> to Jamaica on Friday.

Infinitives (*to* + verb base), on the other hand, are often part of a verb chain, but they are not the main verb (main action) of a sentence:

Angela wants <u>to see</u> that movie.

In this example, *wants* is the main verb; what Angela wants (the action she wants to take) is *to see* the film.

WHEN TO USE INFINITIVES AND GERUNDS

It can be tricky trying to determine whether you should use an infinitive or a gerund after a verb. Here are a few helpful guidelines:

- Always use a **gerund** after a preposition.
  You will save time and money <u>by taking</u> the train.
  He is always frustrated <u>after meeting</u> with his lawyer.

- Always use a **gerund** after the following verbs:

admit	deny	imagine	quit
appreciate	discuss	keep	recall
avoid	dislike	miss	resist
can't help	enjoy	postpone	risk
consider	escape	practice	suggest
delay	finish	put off	tolerate

  I just missed <u>catching</u> that train!
  I am considering <u>joining</u> the Army.
  Sam and Amy are discussing <u>throwing</u> a party for Javier.
  We practiced <u>dancing</u> for weeks before the reunion.

- In general, use an **infinitive** after these verbs:

agree	claim	manage	promise
ask	decide	need	refuse
beg	expect	offer	venture
bother	fail	plan	want
choose	hope	pretend	wish

  I asked him <u>to attend</u> the lecture with me.
  He claims <u>to know</u> the president personally.
  Don't pretend <u>to be</u> someone you are not.
  She offered <u>to help</u> me study for the exam.

■ With a verb + noun/pronoun construct, use an **infinitive** after these verbs:

advise	convince	order	urge
allow	encourage	persuade	want
ask	expect	remind	warn
cause	force	require	
command	need	tell	

> Enron's bankruptcy <u>convinced</u> many <u>companies</u> <u>to diversify</u> their 401K investments.
>
> His mother <u>warned</u> <u>him</u> not <u>to buy</u> that used car.

Study Tips for Verbs and the TOEFL Exam

BECAUSE verbs are the driving force in every sentence, and because verbs can take so many different forms, you can be sure that many questions in the structure section will be about verbs. Here are five tips to help you prepare for those questions:

1. Memorize **irregular** and **troublesome** verb forms.
2. Remember that verbs should be **consistent in tense.**
3. Make sure that verbs **agree** with their subject.
4. Make sure the correct **helping verbs** are used to convey the intended meaning.
5. Use **infinitives** and **gerunds** correctly.

Practice 4

Here are more questions to practice verbs. You will find the Answer Key in Appendix A.

1. After the Grimm Brothers <u>had</u> <u>collected</u> "housewives tales" from around the country, they <u>edit</u> them
                               A   B   C

into stories <u>appropriate</u> for children.
                  D

a. A
b. B
c. C
d. D

2. Ryan <u>ask</u> the question <u>that</u> the rest of us <u>were</u> afraid <u>to ask.</u>
      A   B   C   D

a. A
b. B
c. C
d. D

3. The center fielder <u>catch</u> the ball and <u>threw</u> it to home plate, but the <u>throw</u> <u>was</u> too late.

                           A   B   C   D

    a. A
    b. B
    c. C
    d. D

4. I can't help _____ that we made the wrong decision.
    a. to think
    b. think
    c. thinking
    d. thought

5. If I <u>was</u> a little taller, I <u>could be</u> an astronaut, <u>but</u> I don't <u>meet</u> the height requirement.

          A   B   C   D

    a. A
    b. B
    c. C
    d. D

6. Huey _____ in bed for another hour after the alarm went off.
    a. lie
    b. lay
    c. lied
    d. lain

7. The sun <u>was</u> <u>raising</u> over the mountain when I <u>rose</u> out of bed and <u>sat</u> at the table.

            A   B   C   D

    a. A
    b. B
    c. C
    d. D

8. I expect _____ to the meeting.
    a. to go
    b. go
    c. goes
    d. going

9. The key is _____ on the table under the envelope.

   a. lying

   b. laying

   c. lay

   d. laid

10. Lukas and Elliot <u>said</u> that only one of the solutions <u>make</u> sense, and Evan <u>said</u> he <u>agrees.</u>
                         A   B   C   D

   a. A

   b. B

   c. C

   d. D

11. After Peter <u>breaks</u> his <u>promise,</u> Wendy <u>vowed</u> never <u>to trust</u> him again.
                    A   B   C   D

   a. A

   b. B

   c. C

   d. D

12. The doctor suggests _____ less red meat and more fresh vegetables.

   a. to eat

   b. eat

   c. eaten

   d. eating

13. "What <u>are</u> the <u>value</u> of these jewels?" Kim <u>asked</u> as she <u>held</u> them up to the light.
               A   B   C   D

   a. A

   b. B

   c. C

   d. D

14. I told Henderson that I _____ have the report ready by noon, but things didn't go as I'd planned.

   a. would

   b. could

   c. might

   d. should

Nouns

One of the trickiest things about nouns is remembering whether they are **count** or **non-count** nouns. Count nouns refer to distinct, separate individuals or entities, such as *a toy, an apple, a phenomenon.* Non-count nouns refer to things grouped in a mass rather than separated as individuals, such as *grass, milk, blood, bread.* When we refer to numbers of non-count nouns, we have to do it indirectly, as follows:

> *one blade of grass*
> *three pints of blood*
> *ten loaves of bread*

On the other hand, we can enumerate count nouns directly:

> *one toy*
> *three apples*
> *ten phenomena*

Non-count nouns have other special qualities:

1. They have only one form (singular).
2. They must have a singular verb for agreement.
3. They are <u>not</u> preceded by the word *the.*

As a general rule, the following kinds of nouns are non-count nouns:

- Foods that can be bought in bulk or come in various forms: *bread, butter, fruit, meat, rice, sugar, chocolate.*
- Liquids or natural substances that can change shape, depending upon their container or environment: *milk, water, tea, oil, ice, steam, oxygen, smoke.*
- Materials that can change shape, depending upon what they are used to make: *wood, sand, gold, lumber.*
- Abstractions: *kindness, knowledge, integrity, beauty, time.*
- Groups of items that come in different shapes and sizes: *furniture, clothing, money, garbage, luggage.*
- Games: *chess, tennis, golf, baseball, checkers, marbles.*
- Subjects of study: *history, psychology, literature, physics, economics, politics, statistics.*

Pronouns

Pronouns are very useful; they keep us from having to repeat nouns. There are several different kinds of pronouns and some special rules to follow.

PERSONAL PRONOUNS

Personal pronouns refer to specific people or things and have several forms. They can be either singular (*I*) or plural (*we*); they can be subjects (*I*) or objects (*me*). It's usually clear whether you need the singular or plural pronoun. But knowing whether to use *they* or *them* can be a lot trickier. To determine which form to use, you need to determine whether the pronoun is acting as a subject or an object in the sentence.

SUBJECT	OBJECT
I	me
you	you
he	him
she	her
it	it
we	us
they	them
(who)	(whom)

> *He* hired *me.* (subject / object)
> *I* hired *him.* (subject / object)
> *They* hired *us.* (subject / object)
> *He* is taller than *I* (*am*). (subject / subject)
> *The officer spoke to my sister and* *me.* (object)
> *To* *whom* *am* *I* *speaking?* (object / subject)

INDEFINITE PRONOUNS

Indefinite pronouns, such as *anybody* and *everyone,* don't refer to a specific person. These pronouns are always singular and require singular verbs.

anyone, anybody	everyone, everybody	no one, nobody	
someone, somebody	either, neither	each	one

> *I think* *someone is* *coming.*
> *Everyone has* *a ticket already.*
> *Neither one* *of us* *is* *ready to go.* (Notice "us" is plural, but it is in a prepositional phrase, so it cannot be the subject.)
> *Is anybody* *here?*
> *Nobody has seen* *my wallet.*

PRONOUN AGREEMENT

Just as subjects (both nouns and pronouns) must agree with their verbs, pronouns must also agree with their **antecedents.** An antecedent is the word that comes before the pronoun and which the pronoun replaces. For example, in the following sentence:

Male seahorses carry the eggs in their pouches for two to three weeks.

The word *seahorses* is the antecedent. Therefore, the pronoun that replaces *seahorses—their—*must be plural. The indefinite pronouns above can also be antecedents. They require singular pronouns to follow:

Everyone must bring his or her identification card to be admitted.
Anyone who enters the contest must have his or her advisor's approval.
Neither of the tenants could find his or her copy of the lease.

The following indefinite pronouns, on the other hand, are always plural and require a plural verb:

both   few   many   several

Both of us are going to the show.
Only a few have survived.
Many of the seeds have already sprouted.

They must also have plural pronouns when they function as antecedents:

Both brought their children with them.
Many of the students left their notebooks in the classroom when they ran outside.

Finally, these pronouns can be either singular or plural, depending upon the noun or pronoun to which they refer:

all   any   most   none   some

The noun or pronoun following these indefinite pronouns determine their number. If the noun or pronoun is plural, then the verb must be plural. If the noun or pronoun is singular, then the verb must be singular.

<table>
<tr><td><u>All</u> of the <u>work is</u> done.</td><td><u>All</u> of the <u>tasks</u> <u>are</u> completed.</td></tr>
<tr><td><u>Is</u> there <u>any pie</u> left?</td><td><u>Are</u> there <u>any</u> pieces of <u>pie</u> left?</td></tr>
<tr><td><u>Most</u> of the <u>milk was</u> sour.</td><td><u>Most</u> of the <u>glasses</u> of milk <u>were</u> sour.</td></tr>
<tr><td><u>None</u> of the <u>money was</u> spent.</td><td><u>None</u> of the <u>funds</u> <u>were</u> spent.</td></tr>
<tr><td><u>Some</u> of the <u>fruit was</u> shipped.</td><td><u>Some</u> of the <u>apples</u> <u>were</u> shipped.</td></tr>
<tr><td>(Notice these are noncount nouns.)</td><td>(Notice these are count nouns.)</td></tr>
</table>

TROUBLESOME PRONOUNS

A few pronouns are confusing even for native speakers of English. The **possessive pronouns** *its, your, their* and *whose* are often confused with the contractions *it's (it is* or *it has), you're (you are), they're (they are)* and *who's (who is).* The key to using them correctly is to remember that there is no apostrophe if you want to show possession.

Only use the form with an apostrophe if you mean to have a pronoun *and verb* combination.

<u>It's</u> time for us to say goodbye and head home. (It is time . . .)

<u>It's</u> been three years now since the interest rate has changed. (It has been . . .)

The dog wagged <u>its</u> tail happily. (possession)

<u>Your</u> pager is beeping. (possession)

<u>You're</u> going to have to turn off <u>your</u> beeper. (You are going to . . .)

<u>They're</u> waiting for us at the bus station. (They are waiting . . .)

<u>Their</u> bus arrived right on time. (possession)

<u>Whose</u> Palm Pilot® is this? (possession)

<u>Who's</u> coming to the fundraising dinner? (Who is coming . . .)

The pronouns *who, that,* and *which* are also often confused. Here are the general guidelines for using these pronouns correctly:

- Use **who** when referring to people:
    There is the woman <u>who</u> designed this building.
    The man <u>who</u> bought my car wants to buy my bicycle, too.
- Use **that** when referring to things:
    This is the neighborhood <u>that</u> suffered the worst damage during the riots.
    The printer <u>that</u> earned the highest ratings is out of stock.

- Use **which** when introducing clauses that are not essential to the information in the sentence, *unless* they refer to people. In that case, use **who.**

   Rajesh picked up a copy of Discover, <u>which</u> *is his favorite magazine.*
   The Mississippi River, <u>which</u> *originates in Minnesota, empties into the Gulf of Mexico.*
   Douglas, <u>who</u> *used to sing in the renowned Harlem Boys Choir, lives upstairs.*

Practice 5

Circle the correct choice in the parenthesis in each sentence below. You will find the Answer Key in Appendix A.

1. The news (is/are) on in five minutes.

2. None of these keys (unlock/unlocks) the door.

3. Some of the animals (was/were) moved for the winter.

4. Someone left (her/their) makeup in the bathroom.

5. Remember to give Jane and Rita (her/their) appointment card.

6. Almost anybody can improve (his or her/their) writing with practice.

7. Neither the soldiers nor the sergeant was sure of (his/their) location.

8. The conductor let (he/him) and (I/me) into the club car.

9. Melissa and (I/me) witnessed the accident.

10. The disagreement is between (he/him) and (I/me).

11. I work with Assad more than (she/her).

12. (Its/It's) been a year since (their/they're) last meeting.

13. (Whose/Who's) idea was it to take this shortcut?

14. He is the one (that/who) told me about this restaurant.

15. Please bring me the document (that/which) is on top of the filing cabinet.

16. The clothing (was/were) full of moth holes.

17. We have many different kinds of (tea/teas) from which to choose.

Adjectives and Adverbs

Adjectives describe a noun or pronoun in a sentence. They answer one of three questions about another word in the sentence: *which one? what kind?* and *how many?*

WHICH ONE?	WHAT KIND?	HOW MANY?
that cabinet	*willow* tree	*many* hits
the other tape	*orange* vest	*five* entrances
his first clue	*greedy* partner	*several* reasons

Adverbs, on the other hand, describe verbs, adjectives, and other adverbs. They answer one of these questions about another word in the sentence: *where? when? how?* and *to what extent?*

WHERE?	WHEN?	HOW?	TO WHAT EXTENT?
The car drove *forward*.	Marvin left *earlier*.	She yelled *loudly*.	Royce could *hardly* wait.
Put your luggage *below*.	Hank called *very early*.	Turtles move *slowly*.	Dean *narrowly* missed having an accident.
Look *here*.	We'll do it *tomorrow*.	The loon cried *mournfully*.	She is *still enormously* wealthy.

ADJECTIVES FOLLOWING VERBS

Pay special attention to adjectives that follow verbs. Sometimes an adjective follows a verb, but it describes a noun or pronoun that comes *before* the verb. The following sentences illustrate this. The adjectives are underlined; the noun they describe comes *before* the verb and are boldfaced.

> These **strawberries** taste <u>sour.</u> (sour strawberries)
> Rhonda's **change** of heart seemed <u>strange.</u> (strange change)
> The **pickles** are <u>salty.</u> (salty pickles)

FEWER/LESS, NUMBER/AMOUNT

Use the adjective *fewer* to modify plural nouns or things that can be counted. Use *less* for singular nouns that represent a quantity or a degree. Most nouns to which an *-s* can be added require the adjective *fewer*.

> Our new neighborhood has <u>fewer children</u> (plural noun) *than our old one had.*
> Denise has <u>less time</u> (singular/non-count noun) *to spare than you do.*
> We have <u>less money</u> than we expected.

The fewer your clients, the more attention you can pay to each.

Similarly, use the noun *number* to refer to plural nouns or things that can be counted. Use the noun *amount* to refer to singular nouns.

We underestimated the *number* of hours we would need to prepare. (*Hours* is a plural noun.)
We planned on spending a significant *amount* of time in the waiting room. (*Time* is a singular/non-count noun.)

GOOD/BAD, WELL/BADLY

These pairs of words—*good/well, bad/badly*—are often confused. The key to proper usage is to understand their function in the sentence. *Good* and *bad* are adjectives; they should only be used to modify nouns and pronouns. *Well* and *badly* are adverbs; they should be used to modify verbs.

Helio did a good job, especially considering the pressure he was under.
The condominiums were badly built.
Elizabeth performed very well on the exam.
What a bad haircut—and it cost me $40!

COMPARISONS

Adjectives and adverbs change form when they are used in comparisons. When you compare *two* things, use the **comparative form** (-er) of the modifier. If you are comparing *more than two* things, use the **superlative form** (-est) of the modifier.

To create the **comparative** form, either:

1. add *-er* to the modifier, or
2. place the word *more* or *less* before the modifier.

In general, add *-er* to short modifiers (one or two syllables). Use *more* or *less* with modifiers of more than two syllables.

taller	*less capable*
wiser	*more dangerous*

To create the **superlative** form, either:

1. add *-est* to the modifier, or
2. place the word *most* or *least* before the modifier.

Again, as a general rule, add *-est* to short modifiers (one or two syllables). Use *most* or *least* with modifiers that are more than two syllables.

Angelo is <u>more organized</u> than Reana, but Maurice is the <u>most organized</u> person I know.
This <u>newer model</u> is clearly much <u>safer</u> than the <u>older</u> one.
Amman is the <u>least qualified</u> candidate, but he is certainly the <u>nicest.</u>

DOUBLE COMPARISONS AND DOUBLE NEGATIVES

Be sure to **avoid double comparisons.** Don't use both *-er/-est* and *more/less* or *most/least* together.

Incorrect: *Horace is the <u>most rudest</u> man I know.*
Correct: *Horace is the <u>rudest</u> man I know.*
Incorrect: *These instructions are <u>more clearer</u> than those.*
Correct: *These instructions are <u>clearer</u> than those.*

Likewise, be sure to avoid **double negatives.** When a negative word such as *no* or *not* is added to a statement that is already negative, a double negative results. *Hardly* and *barely* are also negative words. Remember, one negative is all you need.

Incorrect: *The store doesn<u>n't</u> have <u>no</u> nails that size.*
Correct: *The store doesn<u>n't</u> have any nails that size.*
          The store doesn<u>n't</u> have nails that size.
Incorrect: *I <u>can't hardly</u> hear you.*
Correct: *I can <u>hardly</u> hear you.*
          I can<u>'t</u> hear you.
Incorrect: *We do<u>n't</u> want <u>no</u> disagreement.*
Correct: *We do<u>n't</u> want any disagreement.*

Practice 6

Circle the correct choice in the parenthesis in each sentence below. You will find the Answer Key in Appendix A.

1. Patricia looked (tired/tiredly) after the long day.

2. The doctor walked (slow/slowly) out of the operating room.

3. The (amount/number) of work involved does not justify the (amount/number) of people assigned to the job.

4. Phoebe remembers (fewer/less) about the old days than Grandpa does, but Grandpa tells (fewer/less) stories than Phoebe.

5. Pasta does not taste as (good/well) if it is overcooked.

6. This new arrangement works very (good/well).

7. Charlotte is the (younger/youngest) of the twins and the (shorter/shortest) one in the entire family.

8. The decorator chose the (more/most) unusual color scheme I've ever seen.

Correct any errors in the following sentences:

9. I can't hardly understand why we're still waiting.

10. Denise is more quicker than anyone else on the team.

Matters of Clarity and Style

Three grammatical issues can make the difference between clear, smooth sentences and sentences that are clunky and confusing: misplaced or dangling modifiers, parallel structure, and wordiness and redundancy.

MISPLACED AND DANGLING MODIFIERS

Be sure to place words, phrases, or clauses that describe nouns and pronouns as closely as possible to the words they describe. Failure to do this often results in a **misplaced** or **dangling modifier** and a sentence that means something other than what was intended. This is especially problematic with phrases and clauses that work as modifiers. Take a look at the following sentence, for example:

Swinging from branch to branch, I saw the spider monkey.

It's quite obvious that it was the monkey, not the speaker, who was swinging from branch to branch. But because the modifier (*swinging from branch to branch*) isn't right next to what it modifies (*the spider monkey*), the sentence actually says that *I* was swinging from branch to branch. Here's the corrected version:

I saw the spider monkey swinging from branch to branch.

Sometimes these errors can be corrected simply by moving the modifier to the right place. Other times, you may need to add a subject and verb to clarify who or what is modified by the phrase. Here are some more examples of misplaced and dangling modifiers and their corrections:

Incorrect: *My uncle told me about feeding cattle in the kitchen.*
Correct: *In the kitchen, my uncle told me about feeding cattle.*
Incorrect: *Broken and beyond repair, Grandma threw the dish away.*
Correct: *Grandma threw away the dish that was broken and beyond repair.*
Incorrect: *While driving to school, the dog ran right in front of my car.*
Correct: *The dog ran right in front of my car while I was driving to school.*

PARALLEL STRUCTURE

Parallel structure in sentences makes ideas easier to follow and expresses ideas more gracefully. Parallel structure means that words and phrases in the sentence follow the same grammatical pattern. Notice how this works in the following examples:

Not parallel: *Every day I wrote, exercised, and was meditating.*
(Two verbs are in the past tense, one is a past participle.)
Parallel: *Every day I <u>wrote,</u> <u>exercised,</u> and <u>meditated.</u>*
(All three verbs are in the past tense.)
Not parallel: *I am looking for an assistant who is smart, reliable, and will come on time.*
(Two of the characteristics are adjectives while the third consists of a verb phrase and prepositional phrase.)
Parallel: *I am looking for an assistant who is <u>smart,</u> <u>reliable,</u> and <u>punctual.</u>*
(All three characteristics are adjectives.)

Parallelism is important in lists, as in the examples above, and in the *not only/but also* sentence pattern.

He assured me that he not only <u>saved the file,</u> but also <u>created a back-up.</u>
(Each phrase has a past tense verb and a noun)

The failure was caused not only <u>by an unintentional error</u> but also <u>by a deliberate miscommunication.</u>
(Each phrase has a preposition, an adjective, and a noun)

REDUNDANCY AND WORDINESS

Some TOEFL exam questions may ask you to identify or eliminate **redundancy** or **unnecessary wordiness** within sentences. Redundancy is the unnecessary repetition of ideas. Wordiness is the use of several words when a few can express the same idea more clearly and concisely. These two problems typically result from three different causes:

- The use of unnecessary words or phrases.

    Redundant: *The room was <u>red in color.</u>*

    Correct: *The room was <u>red.</u>*

- Unnecessary repetition of nouns or pronouns.

    Redundant: <u>*Thelma she*</u> *ran into her room and slammed the door.*

    Correct: <u>*Thelma*</u> *ran into her room and slammed the door.*

- The use of wordy phrases instead of adverbs.

    Wordy: *He looked at me <u>in a threatening manner.</u>*

    Concise: *He looked at me <u>threateningly.</u>*

The following sentences all have unnecessary repetition or wordiness. Unnecessary words have been stricken:

I returned ~~back~~ to my room after the meeting was over.

Please repeat ~~again~~ what you said.

The waiters and waitresses ~~they~~ really take care of you here.

Fundraising ~~it~~ provides just enough money for us to function.

The circumstances are very delicate ~~in nature.~~

It was a story ~~that was~~ difficult to tell. <u>Correction</u>: *It was a difficult story to tell.*

Practice 7

Rewrite the following sentences to correct any misplaced or dangling modifiers, unparallel structure, wordiness, or redundancy. You will find the Answer Key in Appendix A.

1. Fried in butter, Sylvan likes eggs.

2. At the age of three, Grandpa took me fishing.

3. While barbecuing our steaks, a hungry salesman walked into the backyard.

4. The study focused on the effects of violence on television, in video games, and violent actions in videos with music.

5. She not only voted against the new policy, but also she was hoping to convince others to vote against it as well.

6. The film *Apocalypse Now* it took Joseph Conrad's novel *Heart of Darkness* and set it in Vietnam during the war.

7. I really like to read science fiction and enjoy reading it very much.

8. At Woodstock, Jimi Hendrix played a version of "The Star-Spangled Banner" that was electrifying.

Prepositional Idioms

Prepositions are often one of the most difficult aspects of learning any foreign language. Just as you need to memorize dozens of irregular verbs, you also need to learn these prepositional idioms:

according to	depend on/upon	next to
afraid of	equal to	of the opinion
anxious about	except for	on top of
apologize to (someone)	fond of	opposite of
apologize for (something)	from now on	prior to
approve of	from time to time	proud of
ashamed of	frown on/upon	regard to
aware of	full of	related to
blame (someone) for	glance at/through	rely on/upon
(something)	grateful to (someone)	respect for
bored with	grateful for (something)	responsible for
capable of	in accordance with	satisfied with
compete with	incapable of	similar to
complain about	in conflict	sorry for
composed of	inferior to	suspicious of
concentrate on	insist on/upon	take care of
concerned with	in the habit of	thank (someone) for
congratulate on	in the near future	(something)
conscious of	interested in	tired of
consist of	knowledge of	with regard to

Practice 8

Answer the questions below. You will find the Answer Key in Appendix A. If the question has a blank, choose the *correct* answer to fill in the blank. If the question has four underlined words or phrases, choose the underlined word or phrase that is *incorrect*.

1. I plan to return to school _____.
   a. at the near future
   b. in the near future
   c. on the near future
   d. within the near future

2. Chad is <u>in the opinion</u> that the woman <u>next to</u> the window is <u>fond of</u> him because she glances at him
                   A   B   C
   <u>from time to time.</u>
                 D
   a. A
   b. B
   c. C
   d. D

3. The report is _____ the effects of genetic engineering on food.
   a. concerned about
   b. concerned in
   c. concerned for
   d. concerned with

4. I would like to <u>congratulate you on</u> how well you have <u>taken care of</u> all the matters <u>related on</u> the
                             A   B   C
   reorganization <u>of your department.</u>
                     D
   a. A
   b. B
   c. C
   d. D

5. I hope you know you can always _____ me.
   a. depend in
   b. depend on
   c. depend to
   d. depend with

▶ Putting It All Together: A Structure Practice Quiz

Answer the questions below. You will find the Answer Key in Appendix A. If the question has a blank, choose the *correct* answer to fill in the blank. If the question has four underlined words or phrases, choose the underlined word or phrase that is *incorrect*.

1. The players <u>prepared</u> <u>good</u> for the tournament but <u>performed</u> <u>poorly.</u>
                A   B   C   D

    a. A
    b. B
    c. C
    d. D

2. After the security guard's performance <u>was evaluated,</u> management <u>decides</u> <u>to dismiss</u> her and <u>asked</u> her to turn in her uniform.

    a. A
    b. B
    c. C
    d. D

3. If <u>your</u> not too busy, and I know <u>everyone is,</u> please read and <u>complete</u> this questionnaire.
    A   B   C   D

    a. A
    b. B
    c. C
    d. D

4. Mitch was sure the problem _____
    a. is solve
    b. is solving
    c. was solved
    d. was solven

5. Emmanuel wishes that he _____ never moved from his old neighborhood.
    a. had
    b. did
    c. would
    d. could

6. The plumber <u>did</u> a complete estimate <u>for us</u> so that we <u>would know</u> exactly how much the

              A   B   C

job <u>would costed.</u>

       D

a. A
b. B
c. C
d. D

7. Ginger <u>sees</u> her mother <u>regularly.</u> She <u>was</u> healthy and strong, <u>even though</u> she is over 80 years old.

        A   B   C   D

a. A
b. B
c. C
d. D

8. If the message <u>was</u> more detailed, I <u>would</u> <u>have been</u> able <u>to understand</u> it when I read it.

           A   B   C   D

a. A
b. B
c. C
d. D

9. <u>Half of</u> the textile wall hangings <u>were</u> crooked, but <u>each</u> of the paintings <u>were</u> slightly askew.

    A   B   C   D

a. A
b. B
c. C
d. D

10. <u>Neither</u> Sam nor James <u>wanted</u> <u>their</u> name <u>associated</u> with the project.

    A   B   C   D

a. A
b. B
c. C
d. D

11. The paper is _____ on the dining room table.
   a. lying
   b. laying
   c. lain
   d. laid

12. I think you're the one _____ sent Rachna those flowers.
   a. did
   b. that
   c. which
   d. who

13. <u>Less</u> people attended the conference this year, <u>even though</u> there were <u>more</u> workshops and seminars
       A   B   C
   <u>to choose</u> from.
       D
   a. A
   b. B
   c. C
   d. D

14. This floor <u>doesn't</u> need <u>no</u> more wax; <u>there's</u> plenty <u>already.</u>
                    A   B   C   D
   a. A
   b. B
   c. C
   d. D

15. I really hope _____ to the concert next week.
   a. to go
   b. going
   c. go
   d. goes

16. I don't <u>have</u> <u>anything</u> to wear because my luggage <u>were</u> <u>lost</u> somewhere between California
         A   B   C   D
and Arizona.
  a. A
  b. B
  c. C
  d. D

17. Please <u>remember</u> I am <u>older</u> than <u>him</u> and <u>have</u> more experience.
          A   B   C   D
  a. A
  b. B
  c. C
  d. D

18. He is the opposite _____ his twin sister in nearly every way.
  a. in
  b. from
  c. of
  d. to

19. Jamal read the letter _____.
  a. slow
  b. slowly
  c. in a slow manner
  d. with slowness

20. Ronnel <u>told me</u> that the letter <u>from the attorney</u> was <u>short,</u> curt, and <u>it troubled him.</u>
          A   B   C   D
  a. A
  b. B
  c. C
  d. D

4 ▶ Listening Comprehension

Another key to your success in an American school is listening comprehension. How well can you understand what you hear? This chapter prepares you for the Listening Comprehension section of the TOEFL exam. You will learn exactly what to expect from the exam, including important differences between the computer- and paper-based versions of the test. You will also learn active listening strategies and how you can use them during the exam. Finally, you will find tips for each kind of listening comprehension question and helpful practice exercises.

T GOES WITHOUT saying that your success in college will depend heavily upon your ability to understand what you hear. As carefully as you may read your textbooks, handouts and other course material, you won't do well if you don't comprehend what is said in the classroom. That's why the TOEFL exam includes a section that measures your listening comprehension skills.

▶ The TOEFL Exam Listening Section: What to Expect

The Listening Comprehension section tests your understanding of the kinds of conversations you might hear on an American college campus. While the reading comprehension passages on the TOEFL exam are generally formal, the listening passages are often quite informal and heavily idiomatic. They will typically include expressions and grammatical structures common in everyday speech. For example, you are not likely to see the greeting "What's up?" in a reading comprehension passage. But you might hear something of the sort in one of the passages on the listening test.

On the actual exam, you will hear three types of recorded passages in this section:

- short conversations (Part A on the paper-based exam)
- longer conversations and class discussions (Part B)
- mini-talks and lectures (Part C)

The passages are grouped in these three categories and presented in this order. Thus, you will begin with short conversations (two people speaking), then move into longer conversations and class discussions (two or more people speaking), and finish with a talk or lecture (one person speaking).

▶ Kinds of Listening Comprehension Questions on the TOEFL Exam

You will be asked several different kinds of questions about the passages you hear in this section. They can be divided into the following categories (many of which are very similar to the kinds of questions you will see in the Reading Comprehension section of the exam):

1. **Main topic of conversation.** These questions ask you to identify the main subject of the conversation—who or what the conversation is about. Here's an example:

   Woman 1: *What are the hours for the computer lab? There's no sign on the door.*
   Woman 2: *It's open Monday through Friday, 9 A.M. to 9 P.M., and weekends 10 to 6.*

Question: What are the women talking about?
   a. the location of the computer lab
   b. when the computer lab is open
   c. the best time to use the computer lab
   d. weekend computer lab hours

Answer: b.

Tip: Make sure your answer is the *main* topic—the general subject or issue being discussed. Keep in mind the difference between a main *topic* and a main *idea* (see the next section). Remember that a main topic should be somewhat general. Do not choose an answer that refers to a specific fact or detail from the passage (such as **d.**).

Computer-Based Test vs. Paper-Based Test

ONCE again, there are some important differences between the listening sections of the new computer-based TOEFL exam and the old paper-based exam. The kinds of passages remain the same, but you may be asked fewer questions about those passages on the computer-based test. More important, the questions on the computer exam will be selected according to your level of proficiency. As in the structure section, your first question will be "average" in difficulty. The next question will be easier or harder, depending upon how you answered the first question. The rest of the questions will follow this pattern.

The table below compares the listening sections of the two tests:

Computer-Based TOEFL Exam	Supplemental Paper-Based TOEFL Exam
30–50 questions	50 questions (30 in Part A, 20 in Parts B and C)
Questions are selected based upon your level of proficiency.	All test takers answer the same questions.
Each test taker has a headset with adjustable volume.	The test administrator plays an audiotape for all test takers.
The short conversations begin with a picture related to the conversation. The longer conversations and lectures may include several pictures and visual cues.	There are no pictures or visual cues.
The questions are read aloud on the audiotape and appear on the computer screen.	Test takers hear the questions only. They are not written out.
You control the pace by choosing when to begin the next conversation or lecture. (A clock on the computer screen will indicate how much time you have left for the section.)	All test takers proceed at the same pace and must complete the section within the allotted time. You may not pause the tape.
Some questions may have two answers.	Each question has only one answer.
Most questions are multiple-choice, but some may have special directions, such as sequencing events.	All questions are multiple choice.
Once you submit an answer, you may not change it.	You may return to previous questions and change your answers.

Source: *Barron's Passkey to the TOEFL®,* 4th ed., 2001.

2. **Main idea.** For longer conversations, class discussions, and lectures, you may be asked to identify the *main idea* of the passage—what the speaker(s) are saying *about* the subject. Here's an example of a main idea question based on a short lecture:

> **Professor:** *Next week we will begin our discussion of Mary Shelley's* <u>Frankenstein.</u> <u>Frankenstein</u> *is actually considered by most literary critics to be the first science fiction novel. Understanding what makes this novel a work of science fiction can help you understand why it still has so much power.*
>
> *Science fiction isn't just about space exploration, clones, and robots. Science fiction is any fiction about the realm of possibilities—not just possible futures, but also possible pasts. For example, there's a sub-genre of science fiction called "alternate histories." In these stories, authors explore what our world would be like if history had turned out differently—if the Axis powers had won World War II, for example.*
>
> *In* <u>Frankenstein,</u> *Shelley explores the social and moral repercussions of what might happen if it were possible to bring the dead back to life. She creates a character who discovers the secret of life and "gives birth" to a man made from the corpses of dead men. Then she imagines what might happen afterward.*
>
> *You may be surprised by how little science there is in this science fiction novel. But like the best of science fiction writers, Shelley focuses on the* <u>human</u> *element by exploring what certain scientific and technological advances would mean for our society. In* <u>Frankenstein,</u> *the message is clear: Dr. Frankenstein is playing God, and his delight turns to horror the moment he brings his creature to life because he is unable to accept responsibility for his creation. If we seek glory without considering our responsibilities, Shelley argues, we are headed for disaster.*

Question: What is the speaker's main point?
    a. *Frankenstein* is a science fiction novel.
    b. Alternate histories are a kind of science fiction.
    c. *Frankenstein* is about the possible consequences of a scientific discovery.
    d. Dr. Frankenstein runs away from his responsibilities.

Answer: **c.**

Tip: Remember, the main *idea* is different from the main *topic*. Main ideas say something *about* their subject. They must be general enough to "cover" the information in the entire passage. Thus, choices that are about specific facts or details (such as choice **b**) cannot be the correct answer. See pages 28–31 in Chapter 2 for a review of main idea.

3. **Details.** These questions ask you to identify specific facts or details mentioned in the lecture or conversation. You will only be expected to remember important facts or details from the longer passages. Because the short conversations are so short, however, you may be asked about any detail from the

passage. Here are two examples. The first is based on the lecture above; the second refers to the short conversation about the computer lab.

Question: Dr. Frankenstein discovers:
  a. the secret of life
  b. an alternate history
  c. moral responsibility
  d. a living corpse
Answer: a.

Question: What are the computer lab hours on Wednesdays?
  a. 9 A.M. to 6 P.M.
  b. 10 A.M. to 6 P.M.
  c. 9 A.M. to 9 P.M.
  d. no hours
Answer: c.

Tip: In the Reading Comprehension section, you have the opportunity to use key words from the question to find a specific fact or detail in the passage. Because you only hear the questions *after* you've heard the passages, you don't have the same opportunity in the Listening section. Instead, you have to rely on *listening carefully* and *thinking logically* about the possible answers. At least one should be obviously incorrect and easy to eliminate.

   4. **Idiomatic expressions.** These questions ask you to identify what a speaker means by the use of an idiomatic expression. Here's an example:

   Woman: Jackson said Professor Mellon cancelled the midterm exam.
   Man: Get out!

Question: What does the man mean?
  a. He wants the woman to leave.
  b. They should get out of the room.
  c. He believes the woman is lying.
  d. He is surprised by what the woman said.
Answer: d.

Tip: If you aren't familiar with the idiomatic expression, carefully consider the scenario or situation. For example, would either **a** or **b** be a logical response to what the woman tells the man? Not very likely. You can therefore safely eliminate those two choices. Choice c is also a bit of a stretch, since there's nothing in the conversation to suggest that he thinks the woman is lying.

5. **Recommendations/suggested actions.** These questions ask you to identify what one speaker recommends or suggests to the other speaker. Here's an example:

Man: *I haven't started my essay for American Literature because I've been so busy studying for physics and calculus exams. And the essay is due tomorrow!*

Woman: *Why don't you ask if you can hand in the essay a few days late?*

Question: What does the woman suggest that the man do?
  a. hand his essay in late
  b. talk to the professor about handing the essay in late
  c. not write the essay at all
  d. ask someone else to write the essay
Answer: b.

Tip: Recommendations and suggestions are often signaled by the phrases "you should," "you ought to," "why don't you," or "why not." Listen carefully for these verbal clues.

6. **Inferences based upon tone.** These questions ask you to draw a logical conclusion based upon the tone one of the speakers has used. Here's an example:

Woman: *Henry <u>promised</u> he'd be on time today. I bet he'll be here any second.*

Man: *Sure. Any second!*

Question: What does the man's reply suggest?
  a. He believes Henry will be late.
  b. He believes Henry will be on time.
  c. He has to leave in a second.
  d. He doesn't want to see Henry.
Answer: a.

Tip: A word like "sure" can mean half a dozen different things depending upon the tone the speaker uses—*how* the speaker says it. **Tone** is the *mood* or *attitude* that the speaker conveys about his or her subject. In fact, in speech, more meaning is conveyed by tone than by the actual words used. A word like "sure" is a perfect example. Think of all the ways this word can be said and all the different meanings the variety of tone can convey. During the exam, listen carefully to *how* the speaker says what he or she says. What mood or attitude seems to come across—joy? anger? sadness? excitement? disbelief? Is the speaker making a threat? a demand? a plea?

7. **Inferences based upon details of the situation.** These questions ask you to draw a logical conclusion based upon the specific information provided in the passage. The questions may ask you what a speaker *implies* (suggests), what *problem* a speaker is facing, or what *assumption* a speaker is making. Here's an example:

> **Man:** *So, how'd you do on the physics midterm?*
>
> **Woman:** *Let's just say that I won't be making the Dean's List this semester.*

Question: What does the woman mean?
  a. She got the highest score in the class.
  b. She'll be too busy to be on the Dean's List.
  c. She didn't take the exam after all.
  d. She thinks she did very poorly on the exam.

Answer: d.

Tip: Remember that these questions are different from those that ask you to *identify* specific facts or details. Here, you need to *draw* a *conclusion* based upon those specific facts or details in the passage. What inference can you make based upon the situation or scenario?

8. **Inferences about the future (predictions).** These questions ask you to draw a logical conclusion about what the speaker(s) will do based upon the conversation. Here's an example:

> **Man:** *Oh, no! Look what time it is! If I leave now, I'll still be late for class. It's a 15-minute walk.*
>
> **Woman:** *You will just make it if you take my car.*

Question: What will the man probably do?
  a. Borrow the woman's car and drive to class.
  b. Run as fast as he can to class.
  c. Skip class and stay with the woman.
  d. Call a taxi.

Answer: a.

Tip: Again, you need to draw a logical conclusion here based upon the specific facts and details in the passage. Think about the situation or scenario and the second speaker's response. Really, she's making a suggestion—to borrow her car—though she doesn't explicitly state the offer. See which answer best matches the second speaker's reply.

Other Questions on the Computer-Based Test

All of the questions on the paper-based exam are multiple-choice questions with just one correct answer. Most of the questions on the computer-based test are also multiple choice. But the computer-based exam also includes the following additional types of questions:

1. **Questions that have more than one answer.** A few questions may have more than one possible correct answer. You will be asked to select the options that correctly answer the question. Here's an example:

Question: According to the professor, *Frankenstein* deals with which aspects of science and technology? [Click on two answers.]
   a. fictional impact
   b. social impact
   c. historical impact
   d. moral impact
Answer: b and d.

2. **Questions with visuals.** You will be asked to select an image (a drawing, picture, or chart, for example) that corresponds to or represents information from the passage. Here's an example:

Question: Choose the drawing that best represents how Dr. Frankenstein felt when his creation first came to life. [Click on a drawing.]
Answer: You would choose the picture that shows Frankenstein looking horrified or afraid.

3. **Sequencing questions.** These questions ask you to place information or events in the proper sequence. Here's an example:

Question: The professor describes the four stages of grief. Summarize the grieving process by placing the stages in the proper order. [Click on a word. Then click on the space below where it belongs. Use each word only once.]

depression   acceptance   denial   anger

1 _____
2 _____
3 _____
4 _____

Answer:
   1   denial
   2   anger
   3   depression
   4   acceptance

4. **Classification or matching questions.** These questions ask you to match information by placing facts or sentences into the appropriate categories.

Question: The professor describes Freud's theory of the personality. Match the element of the personality with its definition. [Click on a sentence. Then click on the space where it belongs. Use each sentence only once.]

The part of the personality that is the conscious awareness of the self and is driven by the reality principle.

The part of the personality that is beneath our conscious awareness and is driven by the pleasure principle.

The part of the personality that includes awareness of the self as a member of a larger society; the conscience.

Id	Ego	Superego

Answer:

Id	Ego	Superego
The part of the personality that is beneath our conscious awareness and is driven by the pleasure principle.	*The part of the personality that is the conscious awareness of the self and is driven by the reality principle.*	*The part of the personality that includes awareness of the self as a member of a larger society; the conscience.*

► Listening Strategies

Many people think of listening, like reading, as a passive activity. But you can comprehend much more of what you hear if you listen *actively*. Indeed, knowing *how* to listen can make a tremendous difference in how much is understood.

Hearing versus Listening

The first step to active listening is to understand the difference between *hearing* and *listening*:

hearing: *perceiving sounds with the ear*
listening: *the process of receiving and constructing meaning from an auditory message*

In other words, you can *hear* things without really *listening* to them. Listening means to hear and to *process* that information—to evaluate, analyze, and *understand* what is heard.

Active Listening Strategies

When you listen to someone in person, there are many things you can do to be a more active listener. You can make sure you give the speaker your undivided attention, looking only at the speaker instead of gazing around the room. You can use non-verbal feedback, such as nodding your head or leaning toward the speaker. You can focus on the speaker's message rather than other elements that may be distracting, such as the speaker's appearance. And you can interject questions and "affirmations," such as "yes," "I see," and "really," to acknowledge and help clarify the speaker's message.

But on the TOEFL exam, you won't be face to face with a speaker. Instead, you will be sitting at a table or study carrel, listening to an audiotape. But that doesn't mean you can't be an active listener. You can still:

1. **Concentrate on the speaker.** While you can't look the speaker in the eye, you can still focus on what he or she is saying. Keep your concentration on the conversation or lecture. Don't allow yourself to daydream or drift into other thoughts, such as what you need to get done later in the day. Avoid watching the clock or fiddling with objects.

2. **Use non-verbal feedback.** Even though the speaker can't hear you, you can still nod your head and lean forward "toward" the speaker. These two physical actions may seem too minor to make a difference—especially if the speaker can't see you. But they help to engage your body and mind in the act of listening, and that helps you maintain your focus on the conversation. (And if you are worried about looking silly, don't worry. If you were to look around the testing center, you would probably see many other test takers doing the same thing!)

3. **Focus on the message, not the person delivering the message.** You won't see the speaker(s) face to face, but if you are taking the computer-based exam, you will see pictures of people on the computer screen at the beginning of each listening passage. These images are designed to help orient you to the conversation by giving you a sense of who is talking and the setting in which the conversation or lecture takes place. For example, at the beginning of a lecture, you might see a picture of a professor in a classroom. But these pictures can be distracting. Remember to focus on *listening,* not looking. Concentrate on the conversation, not the picture.

   If you are taking the paper-based exam, find something in the room upon which to concentrate during the reading of each passage—preferably something simple, such as a blank chalkboard, rather than a person in the room. If you focus on a person, you may find yourself thinking about the person's appearance instead of listening to the conversation on the tape. If you find yourself too distracted, simply close your eyes during the reading of each passage.

4. **Use visualization.** Active listening means listening not just with our ears, but also with our other senses. You can use your mind's eye to help you concentrate on the passage and better understand and remember what you hear. When a speaker describes something or someone, paint a mental picture of what you hear. For example, if the professor describes Frankenstein's horror when he first brings his creature to life, in your mind, picture Frankenstein's reaction. What does his face look like? How does he act?

Special Tips for the Computer-Based Exam

BECAUSE the computer-based exam has some features that you won't find on the paper-based test, it's important to be prepared with the right test-taking strategies. Here are a few specific tips for taking the computer exam:

1. **Adjust the volume** on your headset before you begin the listening section. If you can't hear the passages well, you won't be able to perform your best on the exam. You control the volume for your own headset, so make sure it's set at the right level for you before the test begins. You won't be allowed to adjust it once the testing starts.

2. **Don't be distracted by the pictures of people.** At the beginning of most passages, the computer will display an image of the people in the conversation. If you find yourself too distracted by these pictures, take a brief look at the picture, then close your eyes so you can concentrate on the tape. These pictures are for orientation only; they don't reinforce or represent any of the content in the message.

3. **Do pay close attention to other visuals.** As you listen to longer talks and conversations, you may see images such as maps, tables or charts, graphs, drawings, or objects. These are visuals you *should* focus on while you listen. They typically represent information being discussed in the conversation or talk. For example, you might see a graphic representing the three levels of the personality according to Sigmund Freud. This image will help you better understand what the lecturer is describing.

4. **Read the questions on the computer screen as they are being read to you on the tape.** Reading along with the questions can help you better understand what is being asked. And that, of course, can help you better answer the questions correctly.

5. **Keep track of the time.** Because you control the pace of the listening test, it's especially important to keep your eye on the time. Be sure to watch the clock on the computer screen and pace yourself accordingly. Make sure to allow yourself enough time to hear every passage and answer every question.

Listening to Lectures and Longer Conversations

Everyday conversations and class discussions usually have a main point. But it often takes time to get to that main idea, and the conversation may cover many different topics and sub-topics along the way. A lecture, on the other hand, is usually much more organized than a normal conversation or class discussion. And that's good news. While lectures may be long and therefore require extra concentration, they offer many organizational clues that can help you better comprehend what you hear.

MAIN POINT—SECONDARY POINT CLUES

Most lectures are organized around a few main points. These main points are typically followed by secondary or supporting points. These points develop the main ideas with more detailed explanations and specific examples.

A speaker will often announce his or her main points at the beginning of a lecture, as in the following example:

Freud divided the personality into three distinct levels or forces: the id, the ego, and the superego.

This key sentence tells us the main idea and lays out the structure of the lecture (the professor will discuss each of the three levels in turn). To help you distinguish between main ideas and their support, listen for clues. Speakers often use the following phrases to introduce specific examples:

for example	others	furthermore	in part
in addition	for instance	specifically	some

LISTS

Another organizational strategy speakers use is lists. As you listen, be on the lookout for verbal clues like the following:

- *There are <u>four main events</u> that led to the French Revolution.*
- *There are <u>five points</u> that Brauer makes in his argument.*
- *The <u>three symptoms</u> of bipolar disorder are . . .*
- *Animals mark their territory in <u>several distinct ways.</u>*

The introduction to the lecture about Freud's theory of the personality is another good example. The speaker lists the three levels of the personality that she will discuss in the lecture.

KEY WORDS AND CONCEPTS

Speakers also organize their thoughts by key words and/or concepts. These are easy to spot because they are typically offered with a definition or some elaboration of what they mean. The introduction to the Freud lecture, once again, is a good example. The professor lists the three key terms that will be defined and described in the lecture.

Listen carefully for key words and concepts. They will often be unfamiliar words, and the speaker will often immediately follow the word with a definition. Here are some other verbal clues:

"*X*, which means"
"*X*, which refers to . . ."
"This important concept/idea/term"
"This idea is central to *X*'s argument . . ."

▶ The Best Test-Prep Strategy: Listen, Listen, Listen!

The best way—indeed, perhaps the only way—to prepare for this section of the TOEFL exam is to put yourself in situations where English is spoken and **practice active listening.** The more you listen to spoken English, the more you will understand. Go to movies and watch TV shows in English. Go to places like parks and museums where you will hear English being spoken around you. Ask English-speaking friends and relatives to speak to you only in English. The more you practice, the more you will understand. Listen to audio books in English. They are ideal for when you are traveling or exercising, or whenever you have a few extra moments. This will not only improve your listening comprehension but also help you become more comfortable with listening to audiotapes. And there's a wonderful variety of books now available on tape, including both fiction and non-fiction choices.

Practice

To make the most of this practice section, ask someone who speaks English fluently to read the passages, questions, and answer choices into a tape recorder. Be sure your reader speaks at a normal, conversational pace. If that is not possible, read the passages aloud to yourself and answer the questions that follow. You will find the Answer Key in Appendix A.

PART A: SHORT CONVERSATIONS

> Woman: *Roger, is this your notebook?*
> Roger: *No. That looks like Jennifer's handwriting.*

1. What does Roger imply about the notebook?
   a. It belongs to him.
   b. It belongs to the woman.
   c. It belongs to Jennifer.
   d. He doesn't know whose notebook it is.

> Man: *I'm thinking of switching majors. I don't think I'm cut out to be an engineer after all, and for two semesters now English has been my favorite class.*
> Woman: *I'd talk to your advisor before you make any changes.*

2. What does the woman suggest the man should do?
   a. Stick with his engineering major.
   b. Discuss his situation with his advisor.
   c. Switch majors, then tell his advisor.
   d. Double major in engineering and English.

> Woman 1: Are you still coming on the class trip this weekend?
>
> Woman 2: I wish I were, but I can't. I'm totally swamped with work.

3. Why isn't Woman 2 going on the class trip?

   a. She has too much work to do.

   b. She doesn't want to go.

   c. She isn't part of the class.

   d. She is visiting a swamp instead.

> Man: I promised Gabriel I'd meet him after class, but I forgot that I have a meeting with my professor at the same time.
>
> Woman: I have his cell phone number.

4. What will the man probably do?

   a. Get a cell phone.

   b. Call Gabriel on his cell phone.

   c. Postpone his meeting with his professor.

   d. Call his professor on the cell phone.

> Man 1: I'm starving. Let's go get some lunch. How about the pizzeria down the street?
>
> Man 2: I'm more in the mood for some Chinese food. Let's go to Chan's Take-Out.

5. What are the men talking about?

   a. How hungry they are.

   b. How much they like Chinese food.

   c. Where the pizzeria is located.

   d. Where they should go for lunch.

PART B: LONGER CONVERSATIONS AND CLASS DISCUSSIONS

Professor: By now you should all have finished the chapter where Dr. Frankenstein brings his creature to life. I'd like to start by asking you how *you* feel about this event. Yes, Anna?

Anna: I can't believe Frankenstein ran away from his creature. I mean, he didn't even give the creature a chance. He just took off and let this thing loose upon the world.

Professor: How would you describe his reaction? Todd?

Todd: Totally irresponsible. And totally surprising. I mean, he worked so hard to make this happen, right? He stopped eating and sleeping and writing letters to his family all so he could work around the clock on making his creature. And then the minute he succeeded, he ran off.

Professor: Why do you think he did that?

Elena: He was scared. He thought the creature was going to hurt him.

Todd: He was scared, all right, but not so much of the creature.

Professor: Of what, then?

Todd: Of people finding out what he'd done.

Professor: What do you mean?

Todd: Well, I think the minute the creature came to life, and Frankenstein saw what the creature really looked like, he couldn't believe that he'd created such a monster. He wanted to be glorified as a god who could bring the dead back to life, but now he would be seen as a devil who created monsters.

6. What event are the students discussing?
   a. Frankenstein's creation of the monster.
   b. Frankenstein's reaction to giving his creature life.
   c. Frankenstein's arrest for creating a monster.
   d. Frankenstein's discovery of the secret of life.

7. Why is Todd surprised?
   a. He can't believe Frankenstein used dead body parts.
   b. He can't believe the creature tried to kill Frankenstein.
   c. He can't believe Frankenstein would run away after working so hard.
   d. He can't believe Frankenstein kept everything a secret.

8. The students offer two reasons why Frankenstein was afraid. What are those two reasons?
   a. Frankenstein thinks the creature will hurt him.
   b. Frankenstein thinks the creature is dead.
   c. Frankenstein thinks the creature is the devil.
   d. Frankenstein doesn't want people to know he created a monster.

9. From the students' comments, we can infer that Dr. Frankenstein
   a. didn't actually succeed in bringing the creature to life.
   b. didn't consider bringing the creature to life a success.
   c. didn't want anyone else to discover the secret of life.
   d. didn't think about what would happen once the creature actually came to life.

10. The students' attitude toward Dr. Frankenstein can best be summed up by which of the following words?

   a. admiration

   b. horror

   c. indifference

   d. anger

PART C: MINI-TALKS AND LECTURES

The Cold War is one of the most interesting and troubling times in American history. Several important historical events led to the Cold War.

Let's start in 1939, the year that Albert Einstein wrote a letter to President Franklin D. Roosevelt. In that letter, Einstein told Roosevelt that it was possible to create an atomic weapon, and he asked Roosevelt to fund research and experiments in atomic weapons. Roosevelt agreed, and the government created the Manhattan Project, a massive effort to develop nuclear weapons.

Next, the date you all probably already know well: August 6, 1945. The fruit of the Manhattan Project, the atomic bomb, was dropped on Hiroshima, Japan—a civilian, not military, target. An estimated 150,000 civilians were killed in the attack. President Harry Truman and others claimed at the time that dropping the bomb was necessary to force Japan to surrender and end World War II. Others argue, quite convincingly, that we used the bomb largely to show the Soviet Union that we were a superior world power. Though the United States and the USSR were officially allies, tensions between the two countries were already high. A deep ideological battle between the two countries—one Communist, the other Capitalist—was already in place. And each country was determined to outdo the other.

Two years later, in 1947, President Truman established the Truman Doctrine. This important document redefined American foreign policy. It created a "policy of containment" which framed our foreign policy as a battle between "good" and "evil." Of course, we were the good guys, and the Soviets and other Communists were the bad guys. Needless to say, this dramatically increased the growing tension between the two countries.

11. What is the speaker's main point?

   a. The Truman Doctrine created a battle between good and evil.

   b. The tension between the United States and the USSR was caused by World War II.

   c. The Cold War has its roots in several different causes.

   d. The whole Cold War could have been prevented.

12. According to the speaker, Einstein's letter to President Roosevelt:
    a. encouraged research on the atomic bomb
    b. discouraged research on the atomic bomb
    c. expressed doubt that an atomic bomb could be built
    d. expressed a belief that the Soviet Union had already built a bomb

13. According to the speaker, the Truman Doctrine:
    a. improved relations between the United States and the USSR
    b. worsened relations between the United States and the USSR
    c. had no effect upon the relations between the United States and the USSR
    d. angered the American people

14. The speaker describes three events that led to the Cold War. Place these events in proper chronological order.
The Truman Doctrine
Albert Einstein's letter to President Roosevelt
The dropping of the bomb on Hiroshima, Japan
    1.
    2.
    3.

15. The speaker suggests that he believes:
    a. It wasn't necessary to drop the bomb on Hiroshima to end the war.
    b. The bomb should never have been developed in the first place.
    c. Students should already know the events that led to the Cold War.
    d. The Truman Doctrine was a brilliant document.

5 ▶ Writing

Good writing skills go beyond the TOEFL exam—they are essential for success both in school and in the workplace. This chapter tells you what to expect from the TOEFL writing exam and how the writing test is scored. You will learn specific strategies for writing effective essays and six steps for writing well on the TOEFL exam.

IN YOUR MATH classes and perhaps a few other courses, your grade may be based solely on test scores and assignments that require little or no writing. But in most of your other classes, you will have to write—and sometimes write a lot. Your assignments will include essays, essay exams, and short writing tasks of all kinds, such as journal entries and lab reports. Your success in college, therefore, rests heavily on your ability to communicate clearly in writing.

The Structure Section of the TOEFL exam will test your knowledge of English grammar and sentence structure. But even if you know the past tense of "break" and when to use "who" instead of "which," that doesn't necessarily mean you can communicate your ideas effectively on paper. Yes, your sentences need to be clear and grammatically correct. But there's a lot more to writing an effective essay than good grammar. That's why the TOEFL exam includes an essay writing section.

► The TOEFL Exam Writing Section: What to Expect

On the computer-based TOEFL exam, the Writing Section is part of the test; everyone must complete an essay. The paper-based TOEFL exam, however, doesn't include an essay section. The writing test is a separate exam called the Test of Written English™ (TWE®), which is offered in the United States five times a year. The fact that the new computer-based test *requires* all test takers to write an essay reflects just how essential good writing skills are to college success.

While there are some differences between the computer-based writing test and the TWE exam, the task and the test procedures are essentially the same. You will be asked to write a short essay in response to a **prompt**—a general topic and question about that topic. A lot of people are intimidated by essay exams. And on the TOEFL exam, you are not only being asked to write well under pressure—you are being asked to write well in another language. But there's good news about the TOEFL writing exam. First, the essay doesn't have to be long. In fact, because you only have 30 minutes, you are only expected to write about five paragraphs. In contrast, most of the essays you will be assigned in college will require you to write three to five pages. Second, if you are taking the computer-based test, you can view in advance all of the possible writing prompts that you may be given on the TOEFL exam (see sidebar below). There are too many possible topics for you to practice them all, but you can certainly get a good idea of the kind of questions you will be asked, and you can practice with as many prompts as you like. If you are lucky, when you take the exam, you will get a topic that you have already written about.

Essay Prompts Online

TO view the TOEFL computer-based test writing prompts online:

1. Go to www.toefl.org.

2. Click on "Test Preparation."

3. Click on "Writing Topics and Writing Tutorial."

4. Click on "Writing Topics."

The essay prompts are also listed in the *TOEFL Information Bulletin for Computer-Based Testing*.

And here's more good news: On both the computer-based exam and the TWE exam, you are only given one essay prompt. That means you don't have to spend any time deciding which question to answer. You only have to decide *how* you will answer that question. In addition, whatever writing prompt you get on your test, you will be able to answer the question. All of the essay topics are general enough for anyone to write about. None of them will require you to have any kind of specialized knowledge or experience.

On both tests, you will have a half an hour to plan, write, and edit your essay. You will be given a sheet of paper to organize your thoughts before you write. This paper will not be graded, and you can use your native language to brainstorm ideas and outline your essay.

Computer-Based Test vs. Paper-Based Test

AS usual, there are some important differences between the writing section of the computer-based TOEFL exam and the paper-based TWE exam. The types of prompts are the same, but the TWE exam is offered separately from the paper-based exam and at limited times. The computer-based test, on the other hand, requires all test takers to write an essay all on the same day. The table below compares the differences between the two writing tests.

Computer-Based TOEFL Exam	Test of Written English (TWE)
The writing section is a mandatory part of the exam. Everyone taking the computer-based test must write an essay.	The TWE exam is offered only five times each year. If you need to take the TWE exam, you must to select a TOEFL exam test date when the TWE exam is also offered. (There is no additional cost.)
The computer will randomly select an essay prompt for you. Other test-takers may have different topics.	All test-takers have the same essay prompt.
All of the possible writing prompts are listed on the TOEFL® website and in the *TOEFL® Information Bulletin* (see sidebar on page 108).	There is no published list of TWE exam writing prompts.
You have the option of either handwriting your essay or typing it on the computer.	You must handwrite your essay.
The score for your essay is combined with your score for the Structure section. It counts as 50% of your total Structure/Writing score (see Chapter 6 for more details).	Your TWE exam essay score is reported separately from your TOEFL exam score.

Source: *Barron's Passkey to the TOEFL®*, 4th ed., 2001.

► Kinds of Essay Prompts on the TOEFL Exam

On one level, all of the essay prompts on both the computer-based test and the TWE exam are the same. Nearly every question will present you with a statement, situation, or scenario and ask you to take a position and support it. Here's an example:

Some television shows are dramas, some are situation comedies, and some are "reality" shows that deal with real people in real situations. Which type of television show do you prefer? Use specific reasons and examples to support your answer.

As you can see, the topic is general enough for anyone to write about. There's no right or wrong answer; the point is for you to **state your preference** and **explain why** that is your preference.

While the essay prompts are all of this general "take a position" type, they can be organized into five more specific categories:

1. **Agree or disagree with a statement.**

   This is probably the most common kind of essay prompt on the TOEFL exam. You will be presented with a statement and be asked to agree or disagree with that statement. Here are some examples:

   Do you agree or disagree with the following statement? Sometimes, you have to lose in order to win. Use specific reasons and examples to support your answer.

   Do you agree that money is the root of all evil? Use specific reasons and examples to support your answer.

   Do you agree or disagree with the following statement? Schools should require students to wear uniforms rather than wear whatever clothing they desire. Use specific reasons and details to support your answer.

   TIP:

   For example, you might answer the third prompt like this: "Students should not have to wear uniforms, but there should definitely be restrictions on what kind of clothing students can wear."

2. **Take a position and explain it.**

   This is the second most common type of prompt. It asks you to state your position on a general issue. Often the prompt follows this formula: "Some people prefer *X*. Others prefer *Y*. Which do you prefer?" Here are some examples:

   Nowadays, communicating with others is faster and easier thanks to technology like email, cellular phones, and beepers. Has this change improved the way people live? Use specific reasons and examples to support your answer.

   Some people prefer to travel widely and live in faraway places. Others would rather stay close to home and live near family. Which would you prefer? Use specific reasons and details to support your answer.

*What do you value **most** in a teacher—his or her knowledge of the subject, his or her ability to interest you in the subject, or his or her encouragement and support? Which **one** of these characteristics is most important to you? Use reasons and specific examples to explain your choice.*

Some people believe that happiness lies in our accomplishments. Others believe that happiness should come from the steps we take to achieve our goals. In your opinion, where does happiness come from? Use specific reasons and examples to support your answer.

TIP: Be sure to read the question carefully so you can respond appropriately. For example, in the third prompt, your task is to discuss only **one** characteristic. No matter how well you write, your essay will not receive a top score if you discuss all three characteristics or discuss a fourth characteristic instead.

3. **Describe and explain a characteristic.**

   These prompts ask you to identify what you think is an important characteristic or characteristics of a particular person, place, or thing. In the first two types of prompts, you are asked to choose among two or more possibilities (e.g., agree or disagree, travel or stay close to home). With this kind of prompt, *you* get to choose the specific characteristic(s) you would like to discuss. Here are some examples:

   What are the qualities you value most in a friend? Has your opinion about what makes a good friend changed as you have grown older? Use specific reasons and examples to support your answer.

   *People define "success" in many different ways. In your opinion, what **one** quality or characteristic best defines "success"? Use specific reasons and examples to support your choice.*

   What are some of the most important characteristics of a good leader? Use reasons and specific examples to explain why these characteristics are important.

   TIP: Because of the time limit, you can't afford to spend much time choosing the characteristic(s) you will discuss in your essay. Quickly brainstorm some ideas and select the one(s) you will write about. If the prompt asks you to identify more than one characteristic, brainstorm a short list (five to eight characteristics) and then quickly choose the two or three most interesting or important ones for your essay. In a five-paragraph essay, you won't have room to discuss more than two or three characteristics. If you feel confident that you can write more than five paragraphs, then you can add another characteristic.

4. **Respond to a "What if?" situation.**

   Many standardized tests use this kind of prompt. Here, you are presented with an if-then scenario: *If you could X, then what would you do? If X were to happen, then what would you do?* In some cases, the question will be left open. You can respond to the situation in any way (see the first example). In others, you will be given a choice between two possible reactions to the situation. As in the second question type, you will need to choose one of those reactions and explain why you made that choice. Here are some examples:

You have just heard that your local independent grocer may be replaced by a large grocery chain. Would you support this change? Why or why not? Use reasons and specific examples to support your answer.

You have been asked to choose two items to include in a time capsule. What items would you choose for the capsule? Use specific reasons and details to support your answer.

You have recently inherited a significant sum of money with the stipulation that you must donate half of the sum to a charity. To what sort of charity would you give your money? Why? Use specific reasons and details to support your answer.

TIP:

In some cases, you may only be able to choose between two possibilities (for example, to donate to an educational or social services organization). In others, you have limited choices, but you will also have room to impose conditions. For example, you could respond to the first prompt as follows: "I would support the plan if the new grocery store could provide major savings for residents."

5. **Explain a cause or effect.**

These prompts ask you to (1) consider a phenomenon and evaluate its cause(s) or (2) consider a cause and evaluate its effects. You are not expected to provide an expert psychological or sociological answer. Rather, simply use your common sense and personal experiences and observations to respond to the prompt. Here are some examples:

Today, many teenagers have cell phones, beepers, and other means of instant electronic communication. How have these technologies affected the typical teen's behavior? Use reasons and specific examples to support your answer. (Describe **effect.**)

Many people turn on the television as soon as they come into their home. Why do you think some people like to have the television on even if they are not watching a particular program? (Discuss **cause.**)

Reality shows such as Survivor *have become increasingly popular. Why do you think these shows are so successful? Use specific reasons and examples to support your answer.* (Discuss **cause.**)

TIP: Make sure you are clear about whether you need to discuss **cause** (what makes something happen) or **effect** (what happens). Most cause/effect prompts will not limit you to discussing *one* cause or effect, so you can discuss several. But be sure to limit yourself to just a few. Brainstorm a short list, and then choose the two or three most important or interesting causes or effects for your essay. If you feel confident that you can write more than five paragraphs, then you can add another cause or effect to your list.

▶ How the Essay Exam Is Scored

On both the computer-based exam and the TWE exam, each essay is scored by two independent readers. The two scores, which range from 0–6, will be averaged to determine your final essay score. Thus, if one reader rates your essay a 5 and the other a 6, your score will be 5.5.

The two readers do not know the score the other has given your essay. If there is a discrepancy of more than one point (e.g., one reader scores your essay a 4, the other a 6), then a third reader will be asked to rate your essay.

Follow Directions

YOUR essay will score a "0" if you leave the page blank, if you simply copy the topic, if you write in your native language, or if you write on a topic other than what was assigned. **It is extremely important that you respond to the prompt you are given. Do not write about a different topic.**

While scoring an essay is far more subjective than correcting a multiple-choice exam, the Educational Testing Service (ETS®) has developed a detailed **scoring rubric** to guide readers through the essay scoring process. This rubric lists the specific criteria that essays should meet for each score. The complete TOEFL exam "Writing Scoring Guide" is available for your review on the TOEFL® website at www.toefl.org and in the TOEFL® exam bulletin. Be sure to review the scoring guide carefully. The more you know about what is expected of you in the essay, the better you will be able to meet those expectations.

The following rubric has been adapted from the TOEFL Writing Scoring Guide. We have modified the rubric slightly to better fit the writing review in the rest of this chapter.

Sample Scoring Rubric

A "6" essay will:
- respond fully to the writing prompt
- state a clear thesis (main idea)
- provide strong support for or clearly illustrate that thesis through specific reasons, examples, and/or details
- have a logical and effective organization
- develop its ideas thoroughly
- be grammatically clear and correct throughout
- use words and stylistic techniques appropriately
- demonstrate variety in sentence structure and vocabulary

A "5" essay will:
- respond to the essay prompt, but may not address all aspects of the task with equal effectiveness
- have a thesis
- be sufficiently developed (e.g., four or five fully developed paragraphs)
- provide specific reasons, examples, and details to support or illustrate its thesis
- have an overall effective organization
- be grammatically clear and correct throughout most of the essay
- demonstrate some variety in sentence structure and vocabulary

A "4" essay will:
- respond to the essay prompt, but may omit some aspects of the task
- have a thesis, but it may be unclear or insufficiently focused
- be adequately developed (e.g., four solid paragraphs)
- use some reasons, details, and/or examples to support or illustrate its thesis
- have a reasonable organization, though it may not be the most effective or logical approach
- demonstrate less fluency with grammar and usage with errors that occasionally cloud meaning
- have less variety in sentence structure and a more limited vocabulary

A "3" essay will have one or more of the following flaws. It may:
- respond only to part of the prompt
- not have a clear thesis
- be underdeveloped (e.g., only two or three short paragraphs)
- not provide relevant or sufficient support for its thesis
- have a weak or illogical organization
- use words and phrases inappropriately
- have a number of grammatical errors, some of which lead to confusion regarding meaning
- demonstrate a lack of variety in sentence structure and/or vocabulary

A "2" essay will have one or more of the following serious weaknesses. It may:

- lack a clear thesis or focus
- not develop its ideas (e.g., only two short paragraphs)
- provide little or no reasons, details, or specific examples to support its ideas
- offer support that is irrelevant
- be poorly organized (no clear organizational strategy)
- have serious and frequent grammatical errors, often leading to confusion regarding meaning

A "1" essay may have one or more of the following characteristics. It may:

- be incoherent
- be seriously underdeveloped (e.g., only one paragraph)
- have serious and persistent grammatical errors
- use words and grammatical structures incorrectly and inappropriately

A "0" will be given to an essay that:

- is blank
- does not respond to the writing prompt given (discusses a different topic)
- simply copies the writing prompt instead of responding to it
- is written in a foreign language
- is a series of random keystrokes

Write Neatly, Please

THOUGH the quality of your writing should be the only thing that matters, the quality of your handwriting counts, too. If you handwrite your essay, you must write neatly enough for the readers to understand each word. It won't matter how wonderful your essay is if the readers can't understand what you have written.

In addition, like it or not, presentation counts, and the quality of your handwriting can influence your score. The neater your essay, the more favorably readers are likely to look upon what they read. If two essays are of equal strength, but one is written neatly while the other is difficult to decipher, the neater essay may earn a higher score. Untrue as it may be, neat handwriting suggests confidence and control. Sloppy handwriting, on the other hand, may be interpreted as a sign that the writer rushed through the essay and is unsure of his or her thoughts.

▶ Effective Essays and the Writing Process

Experienced writers know that good writing doesn't happen all at once. Rather, it develops in stages. That's because writing is a *process*, not just a *product*. And it's difficult to get a good product without going through each step in the writing process.

The writing process can be divided into three basic steps:

1. Planning
2. Drafting
3. Revising and editing

When you are under pressure to write a winning essay in just a half an hour, you may be tempted to skip these steps and just write your essay in one shot. You *may* end up with a successful essay with this approach. But your chances of doing well on the TOEFL exam writing test—indeed, on any writing task—will increase dramatically if you take the time to work through each step. Even though you only have a half an hour, the five to ten minutes you spend planning and proofreading your essay will be time well spent. In fact, for essay exams, the planning stage is so important that we have divided that stage into four separate steps in the section below.

How to Divide Your Time on an Essay Exam

WHEN your time is limited, how long should you spend on each step in the writing process? On an essay exam, use this general rule of thumb for dividing your time:

¼ of the time: planning

½ of the time: writing

¼ of the time: revising and editing

Your 30 minutes on the TOEFL exam, then, can be divided as follows:

5–10 minutes planning

15 minutes writing

5–10 minutes revising and editing

▶ Six Steps to a Strong Essay

Step 1: Understand the Writing Prompt

Before you can begin to plan your essay, you need to be sure you understand the kind of essay you need to write. As noted earlier, it is essential that you respond accurately to the writing prompt you are given on the exam. If you write about a different topic, you will not receive credit for your essay. It's therefore critical to understand exactly what the prompt is asking you to do.

Though earlier in this chapter we divided the essay prompts into five types, it's worth noting again that they are all essentially the same kind of prompt. They are all designed to get you to state a clear thesis and support that thesis with specific reasons, details, and examples. The writing prompts also have three main parts:

1. A statement, situation, or pair of opposites for you to consider.
2. A question (or questions) for you to answer.
3. Directions for you to follow.

Notice how the following prompts can be broken down into these three parts:

(1-statement) *Nowadays, communicating with others is faster and easier thanks to technology like email, cellular phones, and beepers. (2) Has this change improved the way people live? (3) Use specific reasons and examples to support your answer.*

(1-pair of opposites) *Some people prefer to travel widely and live in faraway places. Others would rather stay close to home and live near family. (2) Which would you prefer? (3) Use specific reasons and details to support your answer.*

(1-situation) *You have been asked to choose two items to include in a time capsule. (2) Which items would you choose for the capsule? (3) Use specific reasons and details to support your answer.*

Some prompts will skip the statement, situation, or pair of opposites and begin directly with a question. Others may include the statement/situation/opposites in the question itself. Notice how this is done in the following examples:

(2) *What are some of the most important characteristics of a good leader? (3) Use reasons and specific examples to explain why these characteristics are important.*

(1 and 2 combined) *Do you agree that money is the root of all evil? (3) Use specific reasons and examples to support your answer.*

(1 and 2 combined) *What do you value **most** in a teacher—his or her knowledge of the subject, his or her ability to interest you in the subject, or his or her encouragement and support? Which **one** of these characteristics is most important to you? (3) Use reasons and specific examples to explain your choice.*

You are on your way to a successful essay if:

1. You understand the statement, situation, or pair of opposites.
2. You answer the question(s) directly.
3. You follow the directions in the prompt. Occasionally, the directions will specify how to answer the question (as in the third example above). Always, the directions will ask you to provide specific reasons, examples, and/or details to explain or support your answer to the question.

Step 2: Formulate a Clear Thesis

Before you begin to write, you need to decide what you're going to write about. Once you are sure you understand the prompt, how will you answer the question it asks? Your answer will form the core of your essay. It will be the main idea that controls everything you write and determine the kind of support you will provide. In other words, your answer to the question in the prompt is your **thesis**—your main idea. It is the "argument" that you are going to make and the idea you need to support.

A thesis does not just repeat or paraphrase the question or prompt. It does not simply make general statements about the topic or state how *others* might respond to the question. A good thesis takes a clear, personal position. For example, take a look at the following prompt:

> *Some people think a good movie is one that makes them think about important problems or issues. Others think a good movie is one that entertains them with adventure, fantasy, or romance. In your opinion, what are the characteristics of a good movie? Use specific reasons and examples to support your answer.*

The following sentences are *not* thesis statements (they do not answer the question):

- There are many different kinds of movies.
- Some movies entertain us while others make us think.
- What makes a good movie?

These, however, *are* thesis statements. They respond directly to the question:

- To me, a good movie is one that both entertains me and makes me think.
- I believe a good movie should first and foremost entertain viewers.
- A good movie is one that somehow addresses important issues.

Practice 1

Formulate thesis statements for three writing prompts listed in this chapter. You will find the Answer Key in Appendix A.

1. _____

   _____

   _____

   _____

   _____

2. _____

   _____

   _____

   _____

   _____

3. _____

   _____

   _____

   _____

   _____

Step 3: Brainstorm Support for Your Thesis

Once you have decided how to answer the question(s) in the prompt, decide how you will **support** your answer. On your piece of scrap paper, list at least three to five reasons, examples, or specific details to support your thesis.

Because you are still in the planning stage, write down whatever comes to mind. You don't have to include everything you list in your essay. And the more ideas you put down, the more freedom you will have to pick the best (strongest) support for your thesis. For example, here's how you might brainstorm support for the movie prompt above:

Thesis: To me, a good movie is one that both entertains me and makes me think.
Why?
like having something to think about
don't like to feel like I wasted time

like getting lost in another world for two hours

Examples:
Crouching Tiger, Hidden Dragon
Planet of the Apes
AI

Brainstorming Strategy: Freewriting

IF you are totally stuck and can't think of how to answer your question or how to support your thesis, try **freewriting.** This brainstorming technique is what it says—free writing. Write down whatever comes to mind about the question or topic. Don't worry about grammar or structure. Write in your own language if you like. Just write. If you keep your hands moving for even two or three minutes, you are bound to come up with some good ideas.

Practice 2

Brainstorm 3–5 supporting reasons, examples, and/or details for the thesis statements you created in Practice 1. You will find the Answer Key in Appendix A.

Thesis 1: _____

_____

_____

_____

_____

Thesis 2: _____

_____

_____

_____

_____

Thesis 3: _____

_____

_____

_____

_____

Step 4: Create a Detailed Outline

The next step is your opportunity to make sure the essay you write is both well organized and well developed. By creating a detailed outline, you can:

- put your ideas in a logical, effective order
- fill in any gaps in your support

BASIC OUTLINE STRUCTURE

Essays follow this basic structure:

- Introduction (states thesis)
- Body (explains and supports thesis)
- Conclusion (brings closure and restates thesis)

Your outline should follow this basic structure, too. Because you are writing a very short essay, you should have at least one point in your outline for each paragraph. The "body" section of your outline should be broken down into the individual supporting ideas for your essay:

1. Introduction
2. Support 1
3. Support 2
4. Support 3
5. Conclusion

Formula for a Great Essay

Introduction: Tell your readers what you are going to tell them. (State your thesis.)

Body: Tell them (Develop your ideas and provide specific support for your thesis.)

Conclusion: Tell them what you've told them. (Restate your thesis.)

ORDER OF IMPORTANCE: YOUR BEST BET

Obviously, you know where to put your introductory and concluding paragraphs. But how do you organize the ideas in the body of your essay? In which order should you present your support?

While there are many different organizational patterns, for the kind of essay you will write on the TOEFL exam, **order of importance** is probably the most effective pattern to use. Because the prompts ask you to take a position (agree or disagree, for example, or decide which characteristic is the most important in a friend), your main support will consist of the reasons that you took this particular stance. A logical and effective way to present those reasons is by rank. Organize ideas from the least important to the most important reason, from the least compelling to the most compelling example.

Order of importance is the structure writers most often use when they are developing an argument. And that's essentially what your TOEFL essay will be: a brief argument expressing and explaining your opinion. The least-to-most important structure works well in arguments because it creates a "snowball" effect. Each idea builds upon the ones that came before it. And when you save your best (strongest) idea for last, your conclusion will have more impact.

Notice, for example, how we might organize the support for the movie essay brainstorming above:

<u>Introduction</u>: I prefer movies that do both.
<u>Thesis</u>: To me, a good movie is one that both entertains me and makes me think.
<u>Body:</u>
Reason 1: I don't like to feel like I've wasted time.
Reason 2: I like getting lost in another world for two hours.
Reason 3: I like having something new or interesting to think about.
Example 1: *Planet of the Apes*
Example 2: *Crouching Tiger, Hidden Dragon*
Example 3: *AI*
<u>Conclusion:</u>
Concluding Statement: As illustrated by my examples, I prefer movies that entertain me and make me think.

Here, the most important reason and the most compelling example come third in each list.

STRONG SUPPORTING PARAGRAPHS

Outlining your ideas not only sets up an effective organization. It can also show you if your essay is sufficiently developed. For an essay to be effective, *each paragraph* needs to be effective, too. And that means each *paragraph* needs to be sufficiently developed.

While there is no magic formula, there are some general guidelines regarding paragraph length. A paragraph with just one sentence—unless that sentence is specifically set off to create a special effect—is too short. It doesn't sufficiently develop its idea. A paragraph with ten sentences, on the other hand, is probably too long. There's likely to be more than one idea developed in that paragraph. (Remember, a paragraph, by definition, is a group of sentences about the same idea.) For an essay of this type, paragraphs of three or four sentences each should be enough to explain and provide specific details and examples for each of your supporting ideas.

To help develop your paragraphs, expand your outline. For each main supporting idea, list at least one specific detail or example. Imagine each paragraph as a mini-essay, with its own thesis (topic sentence) and support (specific examples and details). Notice how the outline above can be expanded as follows:

Introduction:

Thesis: To me, a good movie is one that both entertains me and makes me think.

Body:

Reason 1: I don't like to feel like I've wasted time

    Example: Movies like *Rat Race* or *Home Alone:* funny, but empty, lots of dumb jokes

Reason 2: I like getting lost in another world for two hours

    Detail: This is what I mean by entertaining—not necessarily funny, but captivating

    Example: All three movies below do this—create a new world to explore (planet where apes rule, 18th c? China, the future)

Reason 3: I like having something new or interesting to think about

    Example: All three movies ask interesting and important questions:

    Planet: What if apes ruled over humans? Why do we treat animals the way we do?

    Crouching Tiger: What does it mean to be a woman and to have others define roles for you?

    AI: What makes us human? Can a robot be human if it develops feelings? What does this mean for our future?

Conclusion:

As illustrated by the movies I have discussed, I enjoy movies that not only entertain me for a couple of hours, but that also make me think about the issues raised after I have finished my popcorn and gone home.

Notice now how clearly the order of importance organizational pattern stands out, especially in the last section. And because this outline is so detailed, it offers a guide for just about every sentence in the body of the essay.

Practice 3

Create a detailed outline for one of the prompts for which you brainstormed support. You will find the Answer Key in Appendix A.

_____

_____

_____

_____

_____

_____

_____

Step 5: Write Your Essay

Now that you have a clear, detailed outline, you can begin to write. If you can quickly think of a catchy way to begin your essay, terrific. If not, don't spend precious minutes trying to come up with the perfect opening line. You don't have the time. Remember, you only have 30 minutes for the whole essay—planning, writing, and editing. You need to start writing as soon as you organize your thoughts. One good way to jump right in is to *paraphrase* (repeat in your own words) the statement/situation/opposites stated in the prompt and then state your thesis. Here's an example of this kind of introduction:

> Some people prefer movies that entertain them. Others prefer films that make them think. In my opinion, the best kind of movie is one that does both. I like movies that are entertaining and serious at the same time.

Your introduction should be clear and direct so readers know your thesis and focus. It can also outline your essay by indicating the structure of your essay, as in the following example:

> Today, it's much easier to communicate with others than it was just a decade ago. We can send and receive messages instantly with a number of new technologies. This has improved our lives in many ways by making it easier to coordinate and accomplish tasks, helping families keep better track of their children, and enabling a wider range of people to exchange information and ideas.

Notice how this introduction outlines the three main topics that will be developed in the body of the essay: How new communication technologies (1) make it easier to coordinate and accomplish tasks, (2) help families keep better track of their children, and (3) enable a wider range of people to exchange information and ideas.

Once you have written your introduction, write the body of your essay paragraph by paragraph, following your outline. Make sure each paragraph has a clear topic sentence and specific support. Don't forget about transitions between paragraphs. Key words and phrases like *more importantly, similarly,* etc. help guide your reader through your argument. (See Chapter 2: Reading Comprehension to review transitional words and phrases.)

After your supporting paragraphs, write a brief conclusion. Restate your thesis, *but not in exactly the same words.* Don't introduce any new topics. Instead, make readers feel as if you have covered your topic thoroughly and that they've gotten something meaningful from reading your essay. Here's an example:

> I know I can find plenty of movies that will entertain me, but that alone is not enough. Give me a film that entertains me *and* makes me think. Any movie can entertain me with a zany adventure, a futuristic fantasy, or an endearing romance. But only a *good* movie will also challenge me to think about an important issue.

Step 6: Proofread Carefully

In the three-step writing process, the third step is revise and edit. What exactly is the difference between **revising** and **editing**, anyway?

To *revise* means to carefully read over your essay and make changes to improve it. Revising focuses on improving the *content* (*what* you say) and *style* (*how* you say it). In other words, when you revise, you concentrate on the "big picture": your ideas and how you organize and present them in your essay. Editing, on the other hand, deals with *grammar* (correct sentences), *mechanics* (correct spelling, capitalization, and punctuation), and *usage* (correct use of idioms).

Editing, of course, is very important; your writing should be as clear and correct as possible. But as a general rule, it doesn't make much sense to carefully proofread each sentence only to realize that you need to rewrite several paragraphs.

However—and this is a big "however"—the guidelines are a little different on a timed essay exam, especially when the time is so short. Because your time is so limited, revising—making sure you have a clear thesis that addresses the writing prompt, sufficient and relevant support, and logical organization—should actually take place *before* you write, when you are outlining your essay. You don't have time to rewrite paragraphs or add new ones. But you will probably have a few minutes to change word order, adjust word choice, and correct grammatical and mechanical mistakes. And this final "polishing" step can help make your ideas come across much more clearly for your readers.

Practice 4

Now it's time to practice writing an essay for the TOEFL exam, start to finish. When you are ready, turn the page to see your writing prompt. Give yourself exactly 30 minutes to plan, write, and proofread your essay. Have a piece of scrap paper to brainstorm ideas and outline your essay.

The answer section in Appendix A will provide you with a sample essay for each score 1–6.

Write well!

Practice TOEFL Writing Prompt

Note: Unlike the other prompts in this chapter, this prompt was not taken from the list of possible TOEFL computer-based test essay topics.

Do you agree or disagree with the following statement? *Good things come to those who wait, but better things come to those who go out and get them.* Use specific reasons and examples to support your answer.

You will find the Answer Key in Appendix A.

Notes on the TOEFL Exam: Registration, the Computer-Based Test, Scores, and Tips for Test Day

In this chapter, you will find out how to register for the TOEFL exam and receive and report your score. You will also learn more about the difference between the computer-based and the paper-based exams as well as test center rules and regulations.

AT THIS POINT, you have reviewed the basic skills you need for the TOEFL exam, you know what to expect from each section of the exam, and you know how to effectively prepare for the test. Now it's time to cover a few important administrative matters.

▶ How to Register for the TOEFL Exam

Registering for the TOEFL exam is a relatively easy process. There are two ways to schedule a test date in the United States, Canada, and U.S. territories:

1. Call **1-800-468-6335.** You can use a credit card for payment.
2. Fill out the registration form in the *Information Bulletin for Supplemental TOEFL® Administrations* for the paper-based exam or the *TOEFL® CBT Information Bulletin* for the computer-based exam. Mail your completed registration form to the Educational Testing Service® (ETS®) at the following address:

Educational Testing Service
P.O. Box 6159
Princeton, NJ 08541-6159
USA

To schedule a test date elsewhere, call the Regional Registration Center (RRC) for your area or country. A list of RRCs is printed in the *TOEFL® CBT Bulletin* (see sidebar below). You can also mail or fax a request for an appointment to the RRC in your area using the International Test Scheduling Form from the *TOEFL® CBT Bulletin*.

The TOEFL CBT® Information Bulletin

THE ETS®'s *TOEFL® CBT Information Bulletin* contains important information that you will need to know before you take the computer-based exam. It includes a list of test sites in all countries; institution codes, which you will need to report your scores to the colleges and universities you would like to attend; and other information you will find useful, such as sample questions, test instructions, and a list of writing topics. Request a bulletin as soon as possible if you have not already done so. You can pick up or request a bulletin:

▶ from admissions or international student offices at most colleges and universities

▶ from ETS® representative offices (listed at the end of this chapter and in the *CBT Bulletin*)

▶ from the TOEFL® website, www.toefl.org

▶ by calling the ETS® at 1-609-771-7100.

When to Register

In the United States, the computer-based TOEFL exam is given every day, including weekends, except major holidays. However, it is not given every day at every testing location. Individual locations may offer testing daily, weekly, or monthly, depending upon availability and demand.

Although you may be able to get an appointment for the computer-based test as little as three days in advance, you should schedule your test six to eight weeks in advance in order to register at the center of your choice, since spaces fill quickly. The busiest months are October, November, December, April, and May, so you may want to allow extra time if you are registering in season.

The paper-based test is offered with far less frequency and locations are more limited. At time of publication, the paper-based exam is scheduled on the following days in the 2002–2003 academic year:

- October 19, 2002
- January 18, 2003
- March 14, 2003
- May 10, 2003

Keep in mind that not all of the dates are available at all testing locations. If you plan to take the paper-based test, or if this is the only option you have in your country, call your Regional Registration Center (RRC) well in advance to inquire about available test dates. It is best to call as soon as you realize you need to take the TOEFL exam so you can have a good sense of how much time you have to prepare for the exam.

CANCELING OR RESCHEDULING YOUR EXAM

If your schedule changes and you can't make it to the test you have registered for, you can either reschedule or cancel your test date. If you reschedule, you will be charged a $40 rescheduling fee. If you call to cancel at least three business days before your appointment and fill out a TOEFL exam Refund Request Form, you will receive a refund of $65. In the United States, Canada, or U.S. territories, call 1-800-468-6335 to cancel or reschedule. For testing elsewhere, contact your RRC. The numbers for these centers are listed in the TOEFL® Bulletin and at the end of this chapter.

How Much Does the TOEFL Exam Cost?

THE fee for both the computer-based and the paper-based TOEFL exam in the United States is $110. The fee may be higher for testing centers outside of the country. Check with your RRC for exact fee information.

▶ Computer vs. Paper: The Two TOEFL Exams

There are both positive and negative aspects of the recent changeover to computer-based testing for the TOEFL exam. The good news is that with the computer-based exam, many more test dates are available, and test centers are therefore likely to be much less crowded. You will also have your own headphone set for the exam, and you will be able to get an estimate of your score as soon as you complete the test. If your handwriting is difficult to read, the computer-based test will be helpful, since you will be able to type your essay. You may also find the essay easier to write if you are comfortable composing directly on the computer.

On the other hand, the TOEFL exam is a long one, and concentrating in front of a computer monitor for hours may be taxing. If you have little experience with computers, you may feel intimidated by the computer-based test, even though the exam requires minimal computer skills. Even if you do have computer experience, you may be concerned about your performance on the computer-based test. After all, it's a new program that you will need to get used to. Or perhaps you are not familiar with the English keyboard. But don't worry. You don't need to know how computers work, how to program, or even how to type. You really only need to know how to use a mouse and scroll down a computer screen, and you will have the chance to practice both of these skills using the computer-based exam tutorials available at testing centers and online at www.toefl.org. You may spend as much time as you need practicing with the tutorials at the testing center or online, and you will have the opportunity to practice again immediately before the exam. The tutorials will also help you get used to reading from the monitor and typing. This experience will cut down on your test anxiety and will also be useful throughout your education.

Typing your essay on the computer is optional, so if you are not comfortable keyboarding in English, you can write your essay on paper. If you chose to type your essay, your scores will be available to you sooner. But only choose this option if you can type quickly using an English keyboard and are comfortable composing directly on the computer.

Computer-Adaptive Tests

As you learned in Chapters 3 and 4 of this book, two sections on the computer-based test are computer-adaptive. A computer-adaptive test (CAT) is designed to adjust the level of difficulty of the questions to the performance of the test-taker. This means that if you answer a question of medium difficulty correctly, the next question you get will probably be more difficult. However, if you answer it incorrectly, the next question will likely be easier. You will earn more credit for correctly answering a hard question than for correctly answering an easy question.

As noted earlier, the Listening and the Structure: Grammar and Style sections of the TOEFL exam are computer-adaptive. In these sections, you must answer each question that is presented to you in the order in which it is presented. Unlike the paper-based exam, the computer-based test does not allow you to skip questions, change your answer to a previous question, or see the questions that follow.

Preparing for a Computer-Based Exam

TAKING a computer-based test is a very different experience from taking a traditional paper-based exam. Whether you are comfortable with computers or not, concentrating your attention on the computer screen for hours requires practice. Here are some things you can do to improve your computer skills and performance on the computer-based TOEFL exam:

- Read newspaper or academic articles on the Internet in English. This will help you become more comfortable reading on the computer screen.
- Practice typing your essay on the computer. Use the topics listed in Chapter 5 and in the *CBT Information Bulletin*. Set a timer so you get used to the time limit.
- Practice using the tutorials and other materials from ETS®.
- Get a typing tutorial like the one at www.typing-tutorial.com. There are proper hand and finger positions you can learn that will help you type faster.
- Learn to highlight, delete, copy, and paste text within a document.

Length and Number of Questions

The computer-based test includes a computer tutorial (not timed or scored) to familiarize test takers with the CBT, four test sections, and a break. It takes up to four hours to complete the exam. The paper-based exam, on the other hand, takes two and a half hours, though you will most likely spend an extra half hour to an hour before the test filling out forms and providing identification. You will also need to add an additional 30 minutes if you plan to take the Test of Written English (TWE) exam. There are no breaks during the paper-based exam.

The table below shows how many questions each section of the computer-based test contains and how much time you will have to answer them.

SECTION	TIME LIMIT	NUMBER OF QUESTIONS
Tutorials	no time limit	—
Listening	40–60 minutes	30–50
Structure	15–20 minutes	20–25
Break	5 minutes	—
Reading	70–90 minutes	44–55
Writing	30 minutes	1 topic

RESEARCH QUESTIONS

You may be puzzled by the fact that there is a range of questions and times for each section. That's because not all of the questions are scored. Some questions are included for research purposes only. The ETS® includes these questions to determine whether a new question for a future exam is sufficiently clear.

Don't bother trying to figure out which questions are "real" and which are research questions. Just assume all questions are "real" and do your best on all of them. The time you will have for each section will be proportional to the number of questions, so don't worry that the research questions will hurt you in any way.

▶ How the TOEFL Exam Is Scored

The score on the **computer-based TOEFL exam** ranges from 0–300 and is broken up into sections as follows:

Listening	0–30
Structure/Writing	0–30
Reading	0–30

These "raw scores" are added up, multiplied by 10, and divided by 3 to arrive at your total TOEFL exam score.

The essay is graded on a separate scale of 0–6. This score is combined with the Structure score, accounting for one half of the 30 points for the Structure/Writing section. Each essay is read and scored by two readers. The two scores are averaged, unless there is a discrepancy of more than one point. In that case, a third reader scores the essay to eliminate the discrepancy.

Immediately after the computer-based test, you can get an idea of how well you performed on the exam. You will see your scores for the Listening Comprehension and Reading Comprehension sections. Your Structure/Writing and total scores will be shown as score ranges because your essay is not read and scored immediately.

TOEFL® Test-Prep Materials from the ETS®

THE Educational Testing Service® offers several TOEFL exam study guides and test-preparation materials to help you get ready for the exam. The *TOEFL® Sampler* is a CD-ROM that contains tutorials similar to the ones you will view on the day of the test. *POWERPREP: Software Preparation for the Computer-Based TOEFL®* includes two practice computer-based TOEFL exams. To order these products from the ETS®, call 609-771-7243.

The score on the **paper-based TOEFL exam** can range from 310 to 677. Each section makes up about one third of the total score. If you take the TWE exam, you will receive a separate score for your essay.

There is no passing or failing score on the TOEFL exam. Each institution and program has its own requirements, and you need to find out directly from the institutions you are applying to what the requirements are. Always try to score above the required minimum for admission. A score of 600 on the paper-based TOEFL exam corresponds to a score of about 250 on the computer-based test. Tables in the *TOEFL® CBT Bulletin* contain more information on how the computer-based scores are related to paper-based scores.

Canceling and Reinstating Your Scores

IF after taking the exam you feel that you didn't perform to the best of your ability and that your score is not high enough to get you into the program of your choice, you can cancel your score at the test center, or you can receive a score but decide not to send it to an institution. If you do cancel your scores, they will not be reported to you or any institutions, and you will not receive a refund. After canceling your scores, you will be able to reinstate them within 60 days by sending a written request to:

TOEFL Services
Educational Testing Service
P.O. Box 6151
Princeton, NJ 08541-6151
USA

Your request should include your name, date of birth, daytime phone number, appointment number, and payment of the $10 reinstatement fee. The reinstatement will take approximately two weeks.

► Official Score Reports

You can get one free examinee score report and up to four official score reports to be sent to the institutions of your choice. You must choose those institutions at the testing center or complete a Score Report Request

Form. When you take the exam, make sure you bring the names and locations of the institutions to which you are applying so that you can select them accurately at the test center.

If you take the computer-based test, a printed score report will be mailed to you and the institutions you selected approximately 14 days after the test if you type your essay. If you handwrite your essay, your scores will be mailed to you in approximately five weeks. If you take the paper-based exam, you can expect to receive your results in five to eight weeks after you have taken the test. You should notify the ETS® if, 12 weeks after you have taken the paper-based TOEFL exam, you still haven't received your score.

EXAM	ESSAY	WHEN TO EXPECT SCORES
Paper-based	Handwritten (TWE exam)	Approximately 5–8 weeks
Computer-based	Handwritten	Approximately 5 weeks
Computer-based	Typewritten	Approximately 2 weeks

You can have official score reports sent to institutions other than those you indicate on the day of the test by filling out the TOEFL® Score Report Request Form and paying an additional fee of $12 per recipient. TOEFL® test scores are kept on file for two years after the test date. Scores more than two years old can't be reported.

Scores by Phone

IF you take the computer-based test and can't wait to receive your results by mail, you can find out what your score is over the phone approximately 14 business days after the test date if you type your essay or five weeks after the test if you handwrite it. If you live in the United States, American Samoa, Guam, U.S. Virgin Islands, Puerto Rico, or Canada, call toll-free 1-888-863-3544. From all other locations, call 609-771-7267.

Scores by phone are available seven days a week, between 6 A.M. and 10 P.M. Eastern Standard Time, for a fee of $10 (in addition to any long-distance telephone charges you may incur). When you call, you will need:

▶ a touch-tone phone to provide your 16-digit appointment number

▶ the date you took the exam

▶ your date of birth

▶ a valid major credit card to pay the fee.

How Many Times Can You Take the TOEFL Exam?

You may take the TOEFL exam as many times as you wish, but you are only allowed to take it once in a calendar month, even if you cancel your scores. If you test more than once in a calendar month, your new scores will not be reported and your test fee will not be refunded.

► On Test Day

The Educational Testing Service® is very strict about identification for TOEFL® test takers. If you fail to provide proper registration and identification documents on the day of the test, you will most likely not be admitted to the test center. To make sure your hard work and studying doesn't go to waste because you forgot a piece of paper, collect all the items you are taking to the test in advance and put them in a safe place.

What to Bring to the Testing Center

When you go to the testing center for your exam, you must bring:

For the computer-based exam:
1. **Official identification.** Read the identification requirements in the *CBT Information Bulletin* about acceptable forms of ID. In most cases a passport that has your photograph and signature will do. Your identification will be checked and confirmed before you are admitted.
2. **Your appointment confirmation number.** This will be given to you when you schedule your appointment.
3. **Names of institutions and departments** to which you would like to have your scores sent. At the test center, you will be provided with lists from which to make your selections.
4. **Your CBT Voucher,** if you have one. If you registered for the TOEFL exam via mail rather than telephone, you should receive this voucher two to four weeks after the ETS® receives your CBT Voucher Request Form.

For the paper-based TOEFL exam:
1. **Official identification.** (See #1 above.) Your identification will be checked before you are admitted. It will also be checked at the end of the test.
2. Your **admission ticket** and your **signed photo file record** with a recent photo attached, or official authorization from TOEFL® Services and a recent photo. Glue or tape your photo to the form. Do NOT use staples. Laminated copies or photocopies of your photo are not acceptable.
3. **Institution codes.** If you do not receive your admission ticket, take your list of institution codes with you.
4. **Pencils.** Take at least two sharpened, medium-soft (#2 or HB) black lead pencils and an eraser.

TOEFL® Test Center Procedures and Regulations

On the day of your exam, arrive at the test center at least 30 minutes early to allow time for registration and identification. If you are taking the computer-based exam, you will be assigned a seat in a partitioned area, with a computer, a headphone set for listening to the audio material, and desk space for writing. If you are taking the paper-based exam, you will most likely be seated in a classroom with other students taking the TOEFL exam.

Before and after the test session and at any time you leave and re-enter the testing room, you will be required to write your signature. Your picture will be taken and reproduced on your score report and the monitor you are using if you are taking the computer-based test. If for some reason you have to leave your seat at any time other than the break, raise your hand. Timing of the section will not stop during an unscheduled break.

On the computer-based test, you must answer at least one question in each section and write an essay to receive an official score report. If at any time during the test you believe you have a problem with your computer or need the administrator for any reason, raise your hand. All computer-based testing sessions in the United States are videotaped.

Against the Rules

Here is a list of things you are not allowed to do during the exam or exam breaks. Failure to comply with these rules may result in your dismissal from the test center and canceling of your scores without a refund.

DON'T

- take notes during the Listening and Structure sections.
- bring cellular phones, beepers, pagers, watch alarms, or electronic or photographic devices of any kind to the test center.
- eat, drink, smoke, or chew gum, except as permitted in designated areas of the testing center during break.
- refer to or use any testing materials or aids at any time during the testing session or break. The following are considered to be testing aids: pencils or pens (if you are taking the computer-based test, except for the essay writing section), dictionaries, calculators, watch calculators, books, pamphlets, rulers, highlighter pens, translators, and any other electronic or photographic devices or keyboards.
- leave the test center during the test session and break.
- exceed the time permitted for the break.
- attempt to take the test for someone else or fail to provide acceptable identification.
- create a disturbance or behave inappropriately.
- give or receive unauthorized help.
- attempt to remove scratch paper from the testing room.
- attempt to tamper with the computer.
- attempt to remove test questions (in any format) from the testing room.

Follow these guidelines, and be sure to comply with the test administrator's directions at all times.

Disability Accommodations

IF you have a disability, accommodations for specific conditions will be made, but you must make a request in advance of the test date. Use the Applicant's Request for Nonstandard Testing Accommodations form available in the *TOEFL® Bulletin.* You should also submit a letter of support from a doctor or other qualified medical practitioner, explaining the nature of the disability and the necessary testing modifications to the TOEFL® Disabilities Office at the following address:

TOEFL Disabilities Services

Educational Testing Service

P.O. BOX 6054

Princeton, NJ 08541-6054

USA

Phone: 609-771-7780

Fax: 609-771-7165

TTY: 609-771-7714

▶ Contacting the ETS® about the TOEFL Exam

If you have any questions about the TOEFL exam that are not answered in this book or in the *TOEFL® Bulletin,* you can contact the ETS® at the following addresses and numbers

e-mail:	toefl@ets.org
mail:	TOEFL Services
	Educational Testing Services
	P.O. Box 6151
	Princeton, NJ 08541-6151
	USA
Telephone:	609-771-7100
Fax:	609-771-7500
TTY:	609-771-7714

▶ ETS Representative Offices

In the United States, there is at least one ETS® regional office in each state; heavily populated states, like California, have several centers. To find the closest regional office in the United States, call 800-468-6335. Use this number for regional offices in Canada and U.S. territories, as well.

There are 12 regional ETS® offices outside of the United States and Canada.

AFRICA, EXCLUDING MOROCCO AND TUNISIA

Prometric
P.O. Box 218
Auckland Park, 2006
South Africa
Registration Phone: 27-11-713-0600
Fax: 27-11-482-4062

ASIAN COUNTRIES NOT IN OTHER CATEGORIES [SEE LISTING]

Prometric, BV Branch Office
P.O. Box 12964
50794 Kuala Lumpur
Malaysia
Registration Phone: 60-3-7628-3333
Fax: 60-3-7628-3366

AUSTRALIA, NEW ZEALAND, FIJI, MARSHALL ISLANDS, MICRONESIA, NEW CALEDONIA, NORTHERN MARIANA ISLANDS, SOLOMON ISLANDS, TAHITI, TONGA

Prometric Thompson Learning Pty., Ltd.
P.O. Box 5343
Chatswood, N.S.W. 2057
Australia
Registration Phone: 61-2-9903-9797
Fax: 61-2-9415-3105

EUROPE, FORMER SOVIET REPUBLICS, AND ISRAEL

CITO Group/Prometric
P.O. Box 1109
6801 BC Arnhem
The Netherlands
Registration Phone: 31-26-352-1577
Fax: 31-26-352-1278

INDIA

Senior Plaza, 160-A, Guatam Nagar
Yusuf Sarai:
Behind Indian Oil Bldg.
New Delhi 110049 India
Phone: 91-11-651-1649
Fax: 91-11-652-9741

INDONESIA

The International Educational Foundation/Prometric
Menara Imperium
28th Floor, Suite B
Jalan H.R. Rasuna Said
Metropolitan Kuningan
Super Blok Kav. No 1
12980 Jakarta, Indonesia
Registration Phone: 62-21-831-7304
Fax: 62-21-831-7306

JAPAN

Prometric KK
Kayabacho Tower 15F
1-21-1 Shinkawa
Chuo-ku
Tokyo 104-0033
Japan
Registration Phone: 81-3-5541-4800
Fax: 81-3-5541-4810

KOREA

The Korean-American Educational Commission (KAEC)/Prometric
M.P.O. Box 112
Seoul, 121-600
Republic of Korea
Registration Phone: 82-2-3211-1233
Fax: 82-2-3275-4029

LATIN AMERICA AND CARIBBEAN

Prometric, Inc.
Latin America/Caribbean RRC
3110 Timanus Lane, Suite 200
Baltimore, MD 21244
USA
Registration Phone: 443-923-8160
Fax: 443-923-8569

MIDDLE EAST (EXCLUDING ISRAEL) AND EGYPT, TUNISIA, AND MOROCCO

AMIDEAST/Prometric
P.O. Box 96
Magles El Shaab
Dokki, Cairo, Egypt
Registration Phone: 20-2-337-8973
Fax: 20-2-749-0972

TAIWAN
The Language Training & Testing Center
(LTTC)/Prometric
P.O. Box 23-41
Taipei 106
Taiwan R.O.C.
Registration Phone: 886-2-8194-0200
Fax: 886-2-2363-8840

THAILAND
Institute of International Education (IIE)/Prometric
G.P.O. Box 2050
Bangkok 10501
Thailand
Registration Phone: 66-2-2000-733
Fax: 66-2-6392-706

APPENDIX

A ▶ Answers and Explanations

▶ Chapter 2: Reading Comprehension Skills

Practice 1

1. b. This passage is about the history of bicycles. It does describe several different kinds of bicycles (choice **a**), but these descriptions are in the context of how the bicycle has evolved over time. There is no discussion of how to ride a bicycle, so choice **c** is incorrect. While some of the developments in bicycle design were improved safety features, the passage does not provide information on riding bicycles safely (choice **d**).

2. c. This is the only sentence general enough to encompass all of the ideas in the passage. Each paragraph describes the innovations that led to the modern design of the bicycle, and this design has made it popular around the world.

3. b. The essay describes the history of the bicycle, from its invention in 1818 to its modern design, so "A Ride through the History of Bicycles" is the best title. There is no comparison to other kinds of transportation or any discussion of using bicycles for fitness, so choices **a** and **c** are incorrect. The passage does tell us that bicycles are "one of the most popular means of recreation and transportation around the world." But the focus is on the history of bicycle design, not on its popularity.

4. d. Macmillan may have been a great inventor, but this paragraph only describes his innovations in bicycle design. The first sentence in this paragraph expresses this main idea in a clear topic sentence. The rest of the paragraph provides specific examples of the improvements he made in bicycle design.

5. a. The best clue is sentence 17, which serves as a topic sentence for the paragraph: "With these improvements, the bicycle become extremely popular and useful for transportation." Lawson's improvements may have been innovative (choice **b**), but there is no emphasis in this paragraph on the innovative nature of his design changes (innovation *is* the emphasis in paragraph 3, however). The paragraph also does not focus on the dramatic nature of change over the years (that is the focus of the whole passage, but not this paragraph), so choice **c** is incorrect. The paragraph does mention the popularity of bicycles (choice **d**), but it does not explain *why* bicycles are so popular.

Practice 2

1. b. The main context clue is the word *nervous*. If the speaker is nervous, his voice would not be booming confidently (choice **a**). It is possible that he whispered (choice **c**), but because of the context, it is more likely that his voice was trembling. Choice **d** is meant to mislead, since *quacking* sounds like *quavering*, but there is no reason to expect that he would be quacking like a duck.

2. c. The context clues tell us that the speaker made a mistake by telling Nell about the surprise party. The speaker may be a person who can't keep secrets (choice **a**), but the focus in the passage is on the action (the mistake), not on the person performing the action. Choice **b** (an idea) doesn't make sense in the context of the sentence, since we know an action took place, and choice **d** is similarly incorrect.

3. b. The second half of the sentence tells us that for the Sami, "nature and natural objects had a conscious life, a spirit." The best answer, therefore, is that *animistic* means "the belief that animals and plants have souls."

4. c. *Disturbing* can best be replaced in this sentence with *bothering*. The main context clue is the word *quietly*, which indicates that the Sami did not want to bother the woodland spirits. If they did disturb the spirits, they might make them angry (choice **a**), but the context suggests that disturbing the peacefulness of the woods is first necessary to awaken their anger. Choice **b** does not make sense in the context of the sentence (there is no suggestion that the Sami could hurt the woodland spirits by not moving quietly), and choice **d** can be ruled out because it is a positive word. The context clearly suggests that *disturbing* is something negative.

Practice 3

1. c. This answer is specified in sentence 4. There are three dates mentioned in the second paragraph, so it is important to scan carefully for the correct information.

2. a. This is the only effect not specifically mentioned in the passage. The effects are listed in the second and third sentences.

3. c. This sentence begins "These included machines" and then lists several machines and tools developed during the Industrial Revolution.

Practice 4

1. c. The best place to insert this sentence is after the mention of "the ice age." The sentence to insert begins with "at that time," so it is logical to insert it after a reference to a specific time period.

Practice 5
Part 1

1. 4, 1, 2, 3. *Depressed* has the strongest connotation, while *low* and *down* have much weaker connotations.

2. 1, 3, 4, 2. *Lie* clearly has the strongest connotation, while *fib* and *half-truth* have a much softer connotation.

3. 4, 2, 1, 3. *Life-threatening* connotes the most serious situation, while *risky* merely suggests risk, not necessarily danger or peril.

Part 2
Pair 1

1. Sentence A suggests that the two revolutions had similar causes. The phrase *inspired by* indicates that one revolution looked to the other because of similarities in their situations.

2. Sentence B suggests that the revolutions were similar in method. The phrase *was modeled after* indicates that one revolution used the other as a guide for organizing its own revolution.

Pair 2

3. Sentence A presents bipolar disorder as a more serious condition because it uses the phrase *suffer from* instead of the neutral verb *have.*

4. Sentence B is more objective because it uses more neutral language (*have* instead of *suffer from*).

Comprehensive Practice Questions

1. d. This idea is expressed in the second sentence. Notice how each paragraph describes each type of burn and how it should be treated. Choice **a** is too specific to be the main idea of the entire passage, since it discusses only third degree burns. Choice **b** is too general; the passage describes not just the types of burns but how they should be treated. Choice **c** is also too specific to serve as a net for the passage, since the passage discusses more than just how burns should be treated.

2. d. This fact is stated in the last sentence of the paragraph about first degree burns. Notice that the passage is organized from least to most important (least to most serious type of burn). That should tell you to look early in the passage for details about mild sunburns.

3. a. The question is about third-degree burns, so you should know to look for the answer in the last paragraph. The fourth sentence in that paragraph states that these burns "should not be immersed in water." Be sure to read the question carefully; you're looking for the treatment that is NOT recommended.

4. b. This is the only answer that makes sense in the context of the sentence. If you are unsure, try replacing "it" with each option to see which makes the most sense.

5. d. The context of the sentence suggests that many people believe—wrongly—that butter can help heal burns. The best replacement, therefore, is *popular belief.* Choice **a** is clearly incorrect, because the sentence tells us *not* to apply butter to burns. Choice **b** is incorrect because the context suggests that while an old wives' tale is not true, it is not a direct lie. Rather, it's a mistaken belief. Many old wives' tales are ancient, but putting butter on burns is (erroneous) advice, not a story, so choice **c** is not the best answer.

6. b. Second degree burns are discussed in paragraph 3, and their characteristics are specifically mentioned in the first sentence of the paragraph.

7. d. Choice **a** is incorrect because while the passage offers advice for alleviating symptoms, it does not discuss prevention. Choice **b** is incorrect because much of the passage is about the key similarity between the two types: the same long-term health problem they cause. Choice **c** is too specific to be the main idea of the entire passage. Diet is only discussed in the last paragraph.

8. b. Choice **a** is incorrect because the first sentence of the paragraph tells us there's no cure, so *alleviate* can't mean *get rid of.* Choice **c** is incorrect; certainly no one would be giving advice about how to *increase* the symptoms and problems caused by diabetes. Finally, choice **d** is incorrect because the paragraph describes dietary measures, not medication.

9. b. The second sentence in the third paragraph tells us that the pancreas manufactures insulin. This answer is best found by scanning the middle paragraphs for the word *insulin.*

10. d. Glucose is not a hormone produced by the body but a product of digestion. This answer is best found by scanning the paragraph in which the word *glucose* is italicized.

11. a. The passage tells us that people with diabetes have difficulty processing glucose. The last paragraph also tells us that foods rich in carbohydrates and cooked foods cause blood glucose levels to rise. The passage is suggesting, therefore, that people with diabetes avoid eating too many carbohydrates because their blood glucose levels will be too high and they will be unable to process the glucose. Choice **b** is therefore incorrect, because the suggestion is to avoid extra carbohydrates. Choice **c** is incorrect because it clearly contradicts the information in the passage—diabetes is a very serious disease. Choice **d** is also incorrect. While the last paragraph describes the recommendation that people with diabetes should maintain a normal weight, it does not suggest that people with diabetes *lose* weight. After all, not everyone with diabetes is overweight, and for some, weight loss might increase their health problems.

12. d. Choice a is incorrect because the sentence clearly states that diabetes does not prevent (*interfere with*) digestion. The sentence does not say anything about glucose *triggering* diabetes (choice **b**); rather, it describes the body's inability to use glucose. Choice c is incorrect because the sentence states the opposite—that the body cannot use the glucose produced during digestion.

13. b. The most logical place to insert this sentence is after the sentence that states "nearly half of all people with Type II diabetes do not know they have it." The inserted sentence then makes the important connection between people not knowing that they have the disease and why it's important for people to know that they have the disease.

► Chapter 3: Structure: Grammar and Style

Practice 1

1. Tobias washed his car.
   A. Tobias / washed his car.
   B. The subject is singular.
   C. The predicate is singular.
   D. Tobias washed <u>his car.</u>
   E. There are no indirect objects.

2. My boss gave me a huge raise.
   A. My boss / gave me a huge raise.
   B. The subject is singular.
   C. The predicate is singular.
   D. My boss gave me <u>a huge raise.</u>
   E. My boss gave (me) a huge raise.

3. The engineer measured the water level in the reservoir and tested it for contaminants.
   A. The engineer / measured the water level in the reservoir and tested it for contaminants.
   B. The subject is singular.
   C. The predicate is compound (two verbs: *measured* and *tested*).
   D. The engineer measured <u>the water level</u> in the reservoir and tested <u>it</u> for contaminants.
   E. There are no indirect objects.

4. Horace and Renee both told the detective a different story.

    A. Horace and Renee both / told the detective a different story.

    B. The subject is compound (Horace and Renee).

    C. The predicate is singular.

    D. Horace and Renee both told the detective <u>a different story.</u>

    E. Horace and Renee both told (the detective) a different story.

Practice 2

1. [Since (interest) rates have dropped (considerably) in the (last) month,] it would be wise to refinance the mortgage <u>on your (new)</u> home.

2. I finally reached Tom <u>in his office,</u> and he said he would ship the (redesigned) brochures <u>by</u> (express) mail.

3. [When I mailed the (200–page) manuscript <u>to my editor,</u>] I didn't realize that the pages were (completely) out of order.

4. [Whether you are ready or not,] the (chemistry) test is tomorrow <u>at 9:00</u> <u>in Room 213.</u>

5. The (seven-foot-tall) ostrich is the (fastest two-legged) animal <u>on Earth.</u>

Practice 3

1. c.

2. d.

3. d.

4. c.

5. b.

6. c.

7. a.

8. b.

9. b.

10. c.

Practice 4

1. c. The verbs need to be in the past tense.

2. a. The verbs need to be in the past tense.

3. a. The verbs need to be in the past tense.

4. c. Use gerunds after *can't help.*

5. a. This sentence requires the subjunctive *were.*

6. b. The past tense of *lie* is *lay.*

7. b. The present participle of *rise* is *rising.*

8. a. Use infinitives after *expect.*

9. a. The present participle of *lie* is *lying.*

10. b. The subject of the verb *make* is *one,* so the verb must be the singular form, *makes.*

11. a. The verbs need to be in the past tense.

12. d. Use gerunds after *suggest.*

13. a. The subject of the sentence is *value,* and it requires a singular verb.

14. a. The context of the sentence reflects the speaker's *intention* to have the report ready by noon.

Practice 5

1. is; *news* is a non-count noun.

2. unlocks; *none* requires a singular verb.

3. were; *some* requires a plural verb.

4. her; *someone* requires a singular verb.

5. their; *Jane and Rita* is a plural antecedent.

6. his or her; *anybody* is a singular antecedent.

7. his; the pronoun should agree with the closest antecedent when antecedents are connected with a *neither/nor* phrase.

8. him, me; both of these pronouns are objects in the sentence.

9. I; the pronoun is part of a compound subject in this sentence.

10. him, me; both of these pronouns are objects in the sentence.

11. she; the pronoun is a subject in this sentence (*more than she [does]*).

12. it's, their

13. whose

14. who; the pronoun refers to a person.

15. that; the pronoun refers to an object.

16. was; *clothing* is a non-count noun.

17. tea; *tea* is a non-count noun.

Practice 6

1. tired; the sentence requires an adjective modifying *Patricia.*

2. slowly; the sentence requires an adverb modifying *walked.*

3. amount, number; use *amount* for singular nouns such as *work* and *number* for plural nouns such as *people.*

4. less; fewer; use *less* for references to singular nouns representing a quantity or degree, *fewer* for plural nouns such as *stories.*

5. good; the sentence needs an adjective modifying the noun *pasta.*

6. well; the sentence needs an adverb modifying the verb *works.*

7. younger, shortest; use comparative form (-er) when comparing two items (the twins), and use the superlative form (-est) when comparing more than two items (all of the children in the family).

8. most; use *most* instead of *-est* when the modifier is more than two syllables; assume that the speaker has seen more than two color schemes.

9. Correct sentence: *I can't understand why we're still waiting or I can hardly understand why we're still waiting.* The double negative needs to be removed from the sentence.

10. Correct sentence: *Denise is quicker than anyone else on the team.* The double comparison (*more quicker*) needs to be removed from the sentence.

Practice 7

1. Sylvan likes eggs fried in butter. (Correct placement of modifier.)

2. When I was three, Grandpa took me fishing. *or* Grandpa took me fishing when I was three. (Clarify modifier—who was three?)

3. While we were barbecuing our steaks, a hungry salesman walked into the backyard. (Clarify modifier—who was barbecuing?)

4. The study focused on the effects of violence on television, in video games, and in music videos. (Create parallel structure.)

5. She not only voted against the new policy but also hoped to convince others to vote against it as well. (Create parallel structure.)

6. The film *Apocalypse Now* took Joseph Conrad's novel *Heart of Darkness* and set it in Vietnam during the war. (Eliminate redundant *it.*)

7. I really like to read science fiction. (Eliminate unnecessary repetition.)

8. At Woodstock, Jimi Hendrix played an electrifying version of "The Star-Spangled Banner." (Replace wordy phrase *that was electrifying* with adverb.)

Practice 8

1. b.

2. a.

3. d.

4. c.

5. b.

Practice Quiz

1. b. The sentence needs the adverb *well* to modify the verb *prepared.*

2. b. The verbs need to be in the past tense.

3. a. The sentence requires the contraction *you're* for *you are.*

4. c. The past tense *was* and participle *solved* are required here; the sentence is in the past tense.

5. a. The helping verb *had* is correct.

6. d. The past tense of *cost* is *cost.*

7. c. The verbs need to be in the present tense.

8. a. The sentence needs the subjunctive *were.*

9. d. The pronoun *each* requires the singular verb *was.*

10. c. The antecedent is *neither* and requires the pronoun *his.*

11. a. The sentence requires the verb *lie,* which does not require a subject; the participle is *lying.*

12. d. Use *who* when referring to people.

13. a. Use *fewer* when referring to plural nouns (*people*).

14. b. The sentence has an incorrect double negative.

15. a. Use the infinitive after *hope.*

16. c. *Luggage* is a non-count noun and needs a singular verb (*was*).

17. c. The sentence requires a subject pronoun (*he*).

18. c. Use *of* with *opposite.*

19. b. The sentence requires an adverb to modify the verb *read.*

20. d. The sentence lacks parallel structure; the last part of the sentence should be another adjective (*troubling*) rather than a verb phrase (*it troubled him*).

▶ Chapter 4: Listening Comprehension

1. c. Roger implies that the notebook belongs to Jennifer. He suggests this by saying "That looks like Jennifer's handwriting." Choice **a** is incorrect because the man answers "no" to the question. Choice **b** is illogical; if it was the woman's notebook, she wouldn't be asking Roger if it were his. Roger may not know for sure whose notebook it is (choice **d**), but because he recognizes Jennifer's handwriting, choice **c** is the best answer.

2. b. The woman suggests that the man discuss his situation with his advisor before making a decision. She advises him to talk to his advisor, so choices **a** and **d** are incorrect. She also advises him to talk to his advisor *before* making any changes, so choice **c** is incorrect.

3. a. Choice **b** is incorrect, because Woman 2 says she wishes she could go. Choice **c** is incorrect, because it is not logical for Woman 1 to ask Woman 2 about her plans to go on the trip if she were not part of the class. Choice **d** is incorrect because the idiom *swamped with work* means *overwhelmed with work*; it does not indicate the physical location of a swamp.

4. b. The woman's response indicates that the man can contact Gabriel through his cell phone, so it is logical to assume that that is what the man will do. There is no indication that the man will go purchase a cell phone (choice **a**). The man's concern is that he will keep Gabriel waiting because he must meet with his professor, so it is not logical to assume that he will either postpone his meeting with his professor (choice **c**) or call his professor on the cell phone (choice **d**)—besides, there is no indication from the conversation that he has his professor's cell phone number (or that his professor even has a cell phone).

5. d. The main issue in this conversation is where they should go for lunch. Man 1 proposes one restaurant, while Man 2 proposes another. Only one speaker mentions how hungry he is, so choice **a** is incorrect. Man 2 states that he's in the mood for Chinese food, but that is not the same as saying *how much he likes* Chinese food, so choice **b** is incorrect. Man 1 mentions the location of the pizzeria, but that is not the issue they discuss, so choice **c** is also incorrect.

6. b. The professor starts the discussion by focusing on the chapter where Frankenstein brings his creature to life; the students' responses focus on *how Frankenstein reacted* to this event.

7. c. Todd states that he is surprised because Frankenstein "worked so hard to make this happen . . . and then the minute he succeeded, he ran off."

8. a and d. Elena states that Frankenstein "was scared. He thought the creature was going to hurt him." Todd states that Frankenstein was scared "of people finding out what he'd done."

9. d. It is clear from the conversation that Frankenstein *did* bring his creature to life, so choice **a** is incorrect. There is no evidence from the conversation that Frankenstein didn't want others to discover the secret of life, so choice **c** is incorrect. Choice **b** may seem like a logical answer, but the conversation doesn't suggest that Frankenstein didn't consider *the act* of bringing the creature to life a success. Rather, he didn't consider the *appearance* of the creature a success. In addition, the emphasis in the conversation is on Frankenstein's reactions, so **d** is the best choice.

10. d. The students seem angered by Frankenstein's abandonment of the creature he created. Anna says "I can't believe Frankenstein ran away," and Todd calls Frankenstein's behavior "Totally irresponsible."

11. c. The professor states this main idea in introduction to his lecture when he says, "Several important historical events led to the Cold War." Choice **a** is too specific to be the main idea of the lecture. Choice **b** is incorrect and historically inaccurate. The professor specifically states that during the war, the two countries were allies but that the tension between the two countries was "already high." Choice **d** is an inference that is not supported by evidence in the passage. The professor *does* suggest that the bombing of Hiroshima could have been prevented, but that is not the statement in choice **d**.

12. a. The professor states that Einstein's letter "asked Roosevelt to fund research and experiments in atomic weapons." Choice **b** is incorrect because it contradicts this statement. Choice **c** is also incorrect because the professor also states that Einstein "told Roosevelt it was possible to create an atomic weapon." Choice **d** is incorrect because there is no mention of the Soviet Union in the discussion of Einstein's letter.

13. b. The professor's last statement is that "this dramatically increased the growing tension between the two countries." Choices **a** and **c** are therefore incorrect. There is no indication in the lecture about how the American people reacted, so choice **d** is also incorrect.

14. The correct order is:
1. Albert Einstein's letter to President Roosevelt
2. the dropping of the bomb on Hiroshima
3. the Truman Doctrine

15. a. The speaker states that the argument that the bomb was dropped "to show the Soviet Union that we were a superior world power" is "quite convincing." This suggests that he believes it wasn't necessary to drop the bomb to end the war. This doesn't go as far as to suggest the bomb should never have been dropped (choice **b**), and there's no indication that the professor believes the students should already know this material (choice **c**). Finally, the speaker calls the Truman Doctrine an "important document," but he doesn't suggest that he feels it is a *brilliant* document (choice **d**).

▶ Chapter 5: Writing

Practice 1

Answers will vary. Below are five different thesis statements, one for each type of writing prompt.

1. I do not agree that money is the root of all evil, because sometimes money can be used to do very good things.

2. For me, the most important thing a teacher can do is be encouraging and supportive.

3. I believe "success" is being happy with whatever it is you do.

4. I would put in a copy of the Sunday *New York Times* and a popular magazine like *Parenting.*

5. I think many people like to have the television as a "companion."

Practice 2

Again, answers will vary. Below are brainstorms for the five thesis statements above.

1. not everyone is greedy

money for charities

for art/culture

research for cures for cancer, AIDS, etc.

support education

simply provide necessities for families

2. even if a teacher doesn't know everything about a subject, she can encourage us to learn more about it on our own

encouragement and support builds confidence

confidence is key to learning and doing well in school

a teacher may know everything there is to know about a subject, but if he/she doesn't connect with the students, they may not listen or care

3. whatever you accomplish it doesn't mean anything if you aren't happy

pleasure should be in process as well as product

make your life so that all you do brings you happiness

like your job

live in a place you like

build good relationships

4. NYT would tell all about what's happening in the world

Ads would give a sense of what people liked to buy and how people live

Articles cover all topics, from politics to business to arts

Parents woulds how aspects of human behavior and development

NYT doesn't deal much with issues about kids

5. People who live alone want company

TV is a good substitute; pretend people in their lives

They can get caught up in the characters

If news channel, they want to catch bits and pieces of news when they can

TV on helps them keep from thinking too much, if maybe they're depressed or lonely

Practice 3

Answers will vary. Below is an outline for one of the brainstorms above.

Thesis: For me, the most important thing a teacher can do is be encouraging and supportive.

1. Even if a teacher doesn't know everything about a subject, she can encourage us to learn more about it on our own.
   a. This develops a life-long love of learning.
   b. This teaches students how to find out answers.
   c. Example: 3rd grade, learning about local environmental hazard
2. A teacher may know everything there is to know about a subject, but if he/she doesn't connect with the students, they may not listen or care.
   a. Encouragement and support are evidence of respect. When teachers respect students, students respect teachers and listen.
   b. A teacher who doesn't encourage students may turn them away from subject completely
   c. Example: Mr. Stevens, algebra class
3. Encouragement and support builds confidence
   a. Confidence is key to learning and doing well in school.
   b. Self-confidence is key to success in other areas of life as well.
   c. Example: how Mrs. Wampler helped me build confidence and be a better student

Practice 4

Do you agree or disagree with the following statement? *Good things come to those who wait, but better things come to those who go out and get them.* Use specific reasons and examples to support your answer.

Sample "6" Essay

Growing up, I was always told that "Good things come to those who wait." For a long time, I believed it. But now that I am older, I believe that sometimes it's better to go after what you want instead of just waiting for it.

I think the saying "Good things come to those who wait" teaches us an important lesson in patience. For example, I remember one year when I was about 10, I desperately wanted to go to the beach. I had never seen the ocean before, and it was a long and expensive trip for us. We lived 300 miles from the coast and didn't have a car. My parents kept saying no, we couldn't afford it. They said to wait, that someday we'd go, but not now. I waited all summer and thought for sure it wouldn't happen that year. I had finally resigned myself to waiting until the next summer vacation. But then, the last weekend before school began, my parents surprised us with a family trip to the beach. It certainly was worth the wait.

But that trip didn't just happen for our family. No one came along and just gave us the money or the means to make the trip. I thought then that because I waited, a good thing happened. But now I realize that my parents had to work hard to make that trip a reality for us. They had to save money. They had to postpone other plans they had, such as buying a new washing machine. They had to work overtime. And they had to work hard to find the right places to go and stay so that we could afford the trip.

I've learned that I can make good things happen, too. I recently won an award that included money for college. I never would have won the award just by sitting back and waiting for something good to come my way. Instead, I worked hard in school every day. I always did my assignments and often did extra credit. I studied hard. Now I see the rewards for my hard work. Now I have the grades I need to get into a good college and some of the money I need to pay for that school.

Sometimes, good things do just happen to come along if we are patient. Maybe we just happen to meet the right person or happen to be in the right place at the right time. But I believe that we have the power to make good things come our way. We make choices and set up our circumstances to make it more likely for certain things to happen to us. Good things may come to those who wait, but I believe better things do come to those who go out and get them.

Comments: This essay responds fully to the prompt, providing a clear, strong thesis and strong, relevant support for that thesis. The supporting examples are detailed and logically organized. Each idea is developed thoroughly. There are only one or two minor grammatical errors, and words and stylistic techniques (such as parallelism) are used correctly. The essay demonstrates variety in both sentence structure and vocabulary.

Sample "5" Essay

They say that "good things come to those who wait," and I agree. No matter how much we may "go after" something, a lot of times we just have to wait for the good things to come our way.

For example, just last year I was doing bad in my math class. I wanted very much to improve my grades, and I got help. I worked with a tutor and study extra hard. I did extra work for class and did practicing with my teacher. But I could not get better grades for a long time. I kept trying and trying. Finally, at the end of the year, something happened. I suddenly could understand everything. Finally, my grades began to improve. A good thing came to me after waiting for a long time.

My sister is another example. She is 37, much older than me. She was starting to believe that she never find someone that she'll love, someone to marry her. I kept telling her, be patient, a good thing will come your way if you just wait. She was beginning to lose her patience. She tried all the places where she could meet a good man. She tried different styles and changing her clothes to be more attractive. But nothing worked. Then one day, when she didn't even expect it, she met Lee, and they fell in love. Today they are happily married for more than four years. A good thing came to her when she wasn't even trying.

As you can see from these examples, good things do come to those who wait. Going after what we want can help, but we also need to be patient. It took a long time for my math grades to improve, but eventually they did. It took long time for my sister to find her love, but one day she did. We are both very happy.

Comments: This essay also responds to the prompt and has a clear thesis, and it provides interesting and relevant support. The essay is overall less developed, however, than the "6" essay, offering two supporting paragraphs instead of three. It is well organized. There are some grammar and usage errors, but the errors do not cause confusion for the reader. There is some variety in sentence structure and vocabulary, though the writing and word choice are less sophisticated than in the "6" essay.

Sample "4" Essay

I always believe you have to go after whatever you want in life. That is the only way to get what you want.

Here's example to show you. I always wanted to be champion horseback rider. Of course having horse is expensive. I had to work and work to get a horse and stable. I get up early every morning to ride and take care my horse. For years I work hard and practice. I never give up. Finally, my dream comes true, and I win a big championship. I had a dream and I had went after it.

My brother has similar story. He was always playing piano very good. He wanted to win competitions. He practiced every day for hours. Sometimes we would be sick of hearing him play! But he worked hard and go after his dream. He won even a scholarship to music school. Now he travels around our country playing piano.

So you see, you have to go after what you want. That's the way to get what you want out of life.

Comments: This essay responds to the prompt and has a thesis, but it does not address both parts of the statement. It is less developed than the previous essays. There are two supporting examples, but they are very similar in nature, and the concluding paragraph is very brief and repetitive. The language is less fluent, with more frequent errors in grammar and usage, and there is less variety in sentence structure and vocabulary.

Sample "3" Essay

Some people believe "good things come to those who wait." Other people go after what they want and think its better.

My grandmother always tell me to wait and I will get the good things. I always believe her. One day I find letter that I win scholarship. This for my hard working at the school. I show to my grandmother. She tell me, "See? Good things come to you if you waiting for it."

Going the other side, every day I try to find suitable situation for living in the city. I look and look but find only waste of time with realtors. I decide time for me looking by myself. I go after places like I wanted. Soon I find best for me place in nice part in town. So I get what I want from my going after.

Comments: The essay states the two parts of the statement in the prompt but doesn't state a thesis. The examples do support a position, though—the writer appears to believe that good things come to those who wait *and* one should also go after what one wants. There is no concluding paragraph and there are many grammar and usage errors. There is little variety in sentence structure or vocabulary.

Sample "2" Essay

If waiting, good things coming, better if you going after them. Is true for me. My father he work very hard every day in the store. Working make more money for our family. Trying and trying, and we have bad times somedays. Then we get surprise, money from relative. Everything changing after.

One problem, waiting to long, and nothing come. This is frustration to many people. I find one time too long waiting, I give up. Better to keeping on. Better to be patience.

Comments: This essay does not clearly state or develop a main idea and is seriously underdeveloped. There is one supporting example, but the point of the example is not clear. There are many grammar and usage mistakes, some of which make it very difficult to determine what the writer means.

Sample "1" Essay

Life full of good, even better. People like to go after things. Sometimes waiting, sometimes better. Is no necessary make choosing between that. Both chooses okay. Like cat or dog, red car or blue car. Which better? You depending on it. Sometimes waiting long time for choosing. Ok, giving time for thinking long time about which better.

Comments: This essay (or rather, paragraph) is largely incoherent. It is difficult to determine what the writer means. There is no clear thesis or position and no direct response to the prompt. There are no supporting reasons or examples, and there are serious grammar mistakes in every sentence.

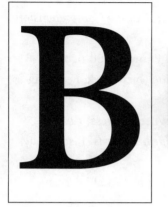

B ▶ Additional Resources

This book has given you a good start on studying for the TOEFL exam. However, as you will find in your future courses, one book is seldom enough. It's best to be equipped with several sources, some general, some more specific.

AS YOU STUDY for the TOEFL exam, be sure to have a good dictionary (English-English, as well as English-your native language) on hand. In addition, you may find it helpful to attend an ESOL (English as a Second or Other Language) class or a TOEFL® test-preparation course. As you work through this book or after you finish, you may also want to use one or more of the following resources, especially as your TOEFL® test date nears.

▶ Listening Comprehension

Art, James and Kraty, Dennis. *Effective Listening Skills* (Columbus, OH: McGraw-Hill, 1995).

Bonet, Diana, Ed., et al. *The Business of Listening: A Practical Guide to Effective Listening* (Menlow Park, CA: Crisp Publications, 2001).

Fox, Grace. *Listening & Speaking Success in 20 Minutes a Day* (New York: LearningExpress, 2000).

Helgesen, Mark, and Steve Brown. *Active Listening: Building Skills for Understanding* (New York: Cambridge University Press, 1994).

► Reading Comprehension

501 Reading Comprehension Questions: Fast, Focused Practice to Help You Improve Your Skills, 2nd edition (New York: LearningExpress, 2001).

Boone, Robert. *What Your Need to Know about Developing Your Test-Taking Skills: Reading Comprehension* (Lincolnwood, IL: NTC/Contemporary, 1995).

Chesla, Elizabeth. *Read Better, Remember More, 2nd edition* (New York: LearningExpress, 2000).

Chesla, Elizabeth. *Reading Comprehension Success in 20 Minutes a Day, 2nd edition* (New York: Learning Express, 2001).

Langan, John. *Ten Steps to Advancing College Reading Skills* (West Berlin, NJ: Townsend Press, 1993).

Morona, Sandra. *REA's Reading Comprehension Builder for Admission and Standardized Tests* (Piscataway, NJ: REA, 1996).

Rudman, Jack. *SAT and College Level Reading Comprehension* (Fort Lauderdale, FL: National Learning Corporation, 1997).

► Writing

Chesla, Elizabeth. *Improve your Writing for Work, 2nd edition* (New York: LearningExpress, 2000).

Chesla, Elizabeth. *Write Better Essays in Just 20 Minutes a Day* (New York: LearningExpress, 2000).

Galko, Francine. *Better Writing Right Now!* (New York: LearningExpress, 2002).

Lerner, Marcia. *Writing Smart* (New York: Princeton Review, 2001).

Lougheed, Lin. *How to Prepare for the Computer-Based TOEFL Essay: Test of English as a Foreign Language* (New York: Barron's, 2000).

Websites

http://owl.english.purdue.edu/—An online writing lab with explanations, workshops and exercises. Many links to other writing help centers. Online tutors available.

http://thecity.sfsu.edu/7.7Efunweb/—A help resource for EFL/ESL students to improve their writing skills.

http://towerofenglish.com—A website to help ESL students and teachers find Web-based resources to learn English.

► English Grammar

501 Grammar and Writing Questions, 2nd edition (New York: LearningExpress, 2002).

Boyne, Matin and LePan, Don. *The Broadview Book of Common Errors in English: An ESL Guide* (Orchard Park, NY: Broadview Press, 1994).

Hopper, Vincent and Craig, R. *1001 Pitfalls in English Grammar* (New York: Barron's, 1986).

Hurford, James. *Grammar* (New York: Cambridge University Press, 1994).

Johnson, Edward. *The Handbook of Good English* (New York: Washington Square Press, 1991).

Kurtin, Mary, Wellman, Laurie and Lim, Phyllis. *Grammar Workbook for the TOEFL Exam* (New York: ARCO, 2001).

Murphy, Andrew. *Grammar Review for the TOEFL* (New York: Harcourt, 1990).

Olson, Judith. *Grammar Essentials, 2nd edition* (New York: LearningExpress, 2000).

Olson, Judith. *Writing Skills Success in 20 Minutes a Day, 2nd edition* (New York: LearningExpress, 1999).

Robinson, Barbara. *Interactive Grammar for Students of ESL* (New York: Cambridge University Press, 1998).

Shaw, Harry. *Errors in English and Ways to Correct Them* (New York: Harper-Collins, 1994).

▶ English as a Second or Other Language

Blusser, Betsy. *Living in English* (Lincolnwood, IL: National Textbook Company, 1989).

Feare, Ronald. *Practice with Idioms.* (New York: Oxford University Press, 1990).

Yates, Jean. *The Ins and Outs of Prepositions: A Guide Book for ESL Students* (New York: Barron's, 1999).

Websites

www.lang.uiuc.edu/r-li5/esl/—A website for ESL speakers/writers, offering help with organization, writing, punctuation, and grammar. Online writing assistants available.

http://iteslj.org/quizzes—Quizzes for ESL speakers/writers, covering slang, holidays, reading, culture, writing, grammar, idioms, and vocabulary. Helpful links to other websites.

http://babel.uoregon.edu/yamada/guides/esl.html—A well-indexed guide to websites for ESL speakers/writers.

▶ TOEFL

Hinkel, Eli. *Barrons TOEFL Strategies* (New York: Barron's Educational Series, Incorporated, 1998).

Matthiesen, Steven. *Essential Words for the TOEFL.* (New York: Barron's Educational Series, Incorporated, 1999).

Phillips, Deborah. *Longman Complete Course for the TOEFL Test: Preparation for the Computer and Paper Test* (Boston, MA: Addison Wesley Longman, 2000).

POWERPREP Software: Preparation for the Computer-Based TOEFL Test (Princeton, NJ: Educational Testing Service, 2000).

Rogers, Bruce. *TOEFL Success 2000: With Cassette* (Princeton, NJ: Peterson's, 2000).

Rymniak, Marilyn and Shanks, Janet. *TOEFL CBT with CD-Rom* (New York: Kaplan, 2000).

Sharpe, Pamela. *How to Prepare for the TOEFL.* (New York: Barron's, 2001).

Sharpe, Pamela. *Passkey to the TOEFL* 4th edition (New York: Barron's, 2001).

Stanley, Nancy and King, Carol. *Building Skills for the TOEFL Test: New for the Revised Test* (Boston, MA: Addison Wesley Longman, 2001).

Sullivan, Patricia, Qiu Zhong, Grace and Brenner, Gail. *Everything You Need to Score High on the TOEFL* (New York: Macmillan, 1998).

TOEFL CBT Success (Princeton, NJ: Peterson's, 2001).

TOEFL Sample Tests 6th ed., available for the paper test and the computer-based test (Princeton, NJ: Educational Testing Services, 2001).

TOEFL Test Preparation Kit with CD-ROM and Cassettes (Princeton, NJ: Educational Testing Service, 2000).

Websites

www.toefl.org—This is the official TOEFL® website from which you can download the TOEFL® Bulletin, find answers to common questions about the exam and order official Educational Testing Service® test-prep materials.

▶ Study Skills and Test-Taking Strategies

Fry, Ronald. *Ace Any Test* (Franklin Lakes, NJ: Career Press, 1996).

Luckie, William R., and Smethurst, Wood. *Study Power: Study Skills to Improve Your Learning and Your Grades* (Cambridge, MA: Brookline Books, 1997).

Meyers, Judith. *The Secrets of Taking Any Test, 2nd edition* (New York: LearningExpress, 2000).

Wood, Gail. *How to Study, 2nd edition* (New York: LearningExpress, 2000).

▶ English Language Arts Skills with Spanish Instructions

Chesla, Elizabeth and Hector Canonge. *Reading Comprehension Success con Instrucciones en Español* (New York: LearningExpress, 2001).

Chesla, Elizabeth and Annette Hertel. *Reasoning Skills Success con Instrucciones en Español* (New York: LearningExpress, 2001).

Meyers, Judith and Ricardo Villa. *Vocabulary and Spelling Success con Instrucciones en Español* (New York: LearningExpress, 2001).

Olson, Judith, and Hector Canonge. *Writing Skills Success con Instrucciones en Español* (New York: LearningExpress, 2001).